VISITS

VISITS

Caring for an Aging Parent:
Reflections and Advice

LEE ANN CHEARNEY

AN AMARANTH BOOK

THREE RIVERS PRESS
NEW YORK

If you have any questions regarding the care of an elder please consult a licensed medical, legal, or financial expert before deciding a course of action.

Copyright © 1998 by Lee Ann Chearney

Published by Three Rivers Press, a division of Crown Publishers, Inc., 201 East 50th Street, New York, New York 10022.
Member of the Crown Publishing Group.

Random House, Inc. New York, Toronto, London, Sydney, Auckland

www.randomhouse.com/

Three Rivers Press and colophon are trademarks of Crown Publishers, Inc.

Design by Karen Minster

Printed in the United States of America

Library of Congress Cataloging-in-Publication Data
Chearney, Lee Ann, 1959–
　　Visits : caring for an aging parent: reflections and advice /
　by Lee Ann Chearney. — 1st ed.
　　　　p.　cm.
　　"An Amaranth book."
　　1. Aging parents—Care.　2. Aged—Care.　3. Adult children—
　Family relationships.　I. Title.
　HQ1063.6.C474　1998
306.874—dc21　　　　　　　　　　　　　　　　　97-28256
　　　　　　　　　　　　　　　　　　　　　　　　CIP

ISBN 0-609-80059-0

10　9　8　7　6　5　4　3　2　1

First Edition

FOR OUR FAMILIES

Acknowledgments

The author gratefully acknowledges the following for their invaluable support and encouragement in the writing of *Visits*: my family, for their courage and determination; my friends, for their unconditional love; the caring, compassionate staff at the Charlestown Retirement Community in Baltimore, Maryland; and the dedicated team of health care professionals who provide the best of care to Mom and Gram, the two I love so much.

FOREWORD

Healing is a matter of time, but it is sometimes also a matter of opportunity.

HIPPOCRATES

Uncovering the life stories and emotional context of the lives of my patients is one special joy of being a geriatrician. Rare is the instance when knowing such information doesn't help me be a better doctor for my patients, rarer still that I come to know the whole story, no matter how hard I dig.

For the last three years I have been the primary physician caring for an older woman named Jessie. I was introduced to her by her granddaughter, Lee Ann, the author of this book, who brought her to see me because Jessie was short-winded. Jessie was concerned because her physician of many years had told her to move to a nursing home. I've come to learn much about Jessie and Lee Ann and other members of their family since that first meeting, and I thought I had a reasonably clear picture of the emotional landscape.

After reading this book, I learned that while I knew many of the facts, and had intuited others correctly, in truth, I only had a rough sketch of the terrain. *Visits* paints a full and immensely rich canvas and gives texture, depth, nuance, and shape to the emotional experience of planning for the care of—and caring for—aging loved ones. It is inspirational, practical, and filled with the sort of wisdom that will be of enormous assistance to anyone making a similar journey.

Bruce Leff, M.D.,
Assistant Professor of Geriatric Medicine and Gerontology,
Johns Hopkins School of Medicine

INTRODUCTION

~

Today, there are fifteen million Americans over the age of seventy-five; in thirty years, there will be twenty-five million. In fifty years, more than one million people will reach the age of one hundred or more. Increasingly, we are taking care of our parents as they age and grow infirm, nursing them through sometimes devastating terminal illnesses. Medical technology has transformed the aging experience, and we are the first generation to grapple with the effects—emotional, financial, and medical—as we care for our aging parents. We are looking for signposts to guide us as we make this difficult life-passage with our mother, father, or grandparents.

Visits is a book of meditations, affirmations, experiences, and advice to comfort and counsel us as we face the challenges of caregiving for the elders who once nurtured and cared for us. Juggling careers and families, we now find ourselves caring for Mom and Dad as well. The roles blur as we shift between the identities of adult and child, wondering sometimes whose hand is the one holding and whose is held: Should Dad drive the car anymore? Why doesn't Mom just order from those convenient catalogs I gave her instead of waiting for someone (me!) to take her out shopping? How can I convince my grandparents that using the stairs can be dangerous? What is the difference between independent living, assisted living, and nursing home facilities? When will Gram realize she needs to let someone handle her finances for her? Why can't I lift Pop's depression? How will I handle it when Mom's Alzheimer's goes so far that she doesn't remember me anymore?

The experience of caring for a parent can be isolating and emotionally powerful, guilt-ridden and frustrating. Not able to reverse the decline of our parents, we can feel like Sisyphus—forever working to preserve a parent's autonomy, only to see the equilibrium shift back to dependency. Both children and parents struggle with the logistical problems of "What can be done?" while simultaneously facing complex changes in our relationship to one another. And we go through it all without realizing our experience is a common one shared with thousands of other children and parents who are going through the same process, confronting the same challenges, every day.

Family relationships, particularly between women—the ones who are the family's nurturing strength and, most often, its caregivers—generate a lasting bond that helps us to understand who we are. According to Susan J. Blumenthal, M.D., M.P.A., deputy assistant secretary for health and assistant surgeon general, one in seven American women is now caring for an aging, chronically ill, or disabled family member. At thirty-eight, I am the long-distance caregiver for my mother, Gloria, sixty-five, diagnosed with Parkinson's disease. I've accompanied Mom on her late-life journey as the two of us attempted to support her autonomous life in her own home with the help of friends, relatives, and community caregiving resources. When, finally, it became unsafe for Mom to continue living in her home, we faced the difficult (seemingly impossible!) decision to sell the house on Kirkwood Road, and Mom moved into an apartment at Charlestown, a retirement community in Baltimore. Providing three levels of care—independent living apartments, an assisted living dormitory, and a nursing home facility—the community seemed ideal to support Mom over the years as her illness progressed and greater levels of care became necessary. Mom is now in the nursing home at Charlestown. With my brother, Mike, I am the co-caregiver for our grandmother, Jessie, eighty-eight, who still lives, indefatigably, independently in her own home in Baltimore.

I have written this book in the hopes that my own experiences in navigating this territory with Mom, Mike, and Gram might resonate with your experiences of caring for your aging parent or grandparent, providing in the words an embrace of comfort, advice, and encouragement that might help you along your way. Every choice in an elder's care is an emotional one. The relationship between parent and child enters a new territory from which there is no turning back.

I have felt the despair of watching someone I love decline with age and illness. And I have learned the incredible joy and strength that comes from loving through life's adversities. Many times in the course of my mother's illness, I wondered what good could come from such a difficult experience. As each obstacle placed in front of us grew larger, seemed heavier and more unmovable, I looked for the seeds of any opportunity to grow through our situation, to find something life-affirming in the midst of it all.

Visits, for me, is a way to bring a healing to my mother's life, and to my own. I have found strength in the telling of my family's stories. Our stories, our experiences, are rich and precious cloth, woven through generations into wondrous, unforeseen, and beautiful patterns. We must embrace our experiences of caring for our parents and grandparents and honor the lessons they have to teach us. By finding the courage to share our experiences openly with others, we grow toward a consensus, building a common foundation for care that shapes the very path we travel. We need to recognize that as individuals, and as a group, our actions will determine the nature and quality of long-term health care in this country. With our parents, we are the ones who will set the signposts as our nation grapples with what it means to grow old at the dawn of a new century.

Our visits with our parents are poignant, difficult; in a moment, they can change us. *Visits* is for all of us who share the journey.

Lee Ann Chearney

VISITS

HUGGING THE SHORE

The waves echo behind me. . . . But there are other beaches to explore.
There are more shells to find. This is only the beginning.

ANNE MORROW LINDBERGH, *GIFT FROM THE SEA*

Like my father, I did not learn to swim until I became an adult. As a girl, hugging the shoreline, zigzagging to put barely a toe in the surf, I followed my father on long walks to gather seashells. He liked them all—some smooth and pink-thin, perfectly shaped; others jagged and black, chalky to the touch. I carried the shells for him in a towel, never looking back to where my mom and brother bodysurfed for hours and raced the big waves to the shore. Mom only let us bring home the best ones. Later, in a ceremony ours alone, my father and I would carry the rest back to the sea, holding hands at the edge of the ocean.

Dad is gone a long time now, but Mom and I both hold onto his shells, saving them in special places. As a woman, I learned to sail in a twelve-foot wooden sailboat christened *Spirit*, still more comfortable near the water than in it. I scan the shoreline for the shell-seekers and ride the swells that carry treasure to shore.

Courage can come from the smallest of treasures.

OLD PEOPLE

*Paradoxical as it may seem, to believe in youth is to look backward;
to look forward we must believe in age.*

DOROTHY PARKER

I must say I had some trepidation about spending so much time with so many old people. Like someone forced to spend vacation with a dowager aunt, I dreaded the prospect of visits to the retirement community at the same time I encouraged Mom about how much fun she'd have living there. "That place is full of old people," Mom would say every time we talked about what we'd do when she couldn't live at home by herself any more. I couldn't disagree with her. Mom was sixty-two when she moved into the retirement community, a good ten years younger than the average resident. But with the symptoms of the Parkinson's becoming stronger, the retirement community seemed the best environment to support her independence.

We couldn't have been more wrong about old people. I've come to love asking these people about their lives. What stories they tell. At first their life stories seemed so incongruous compared with current appearances. But I've learned now that each time I look into an old set of eyes there's so much there to discover. And with all their varied life experiences, these old people all share one thing in common: They survived. They survived risk, boredom, joy, pain, every circumstance—for better and for worse. When I look at them I am not so afraid of getting old—what a ride, every minute unpredictable! Every moment an opportunity.

Age is a beacon to youth, a lifeline of vitality.

PASSAGES

*The man who views the world at fifty the same as he did
at twenty has wasted thirty years of his life.*

As we move from one life passage to another, our situations change, our surroundings change, our bodies change—why not our outlooks? We all share common life passages that mark the times of our lives: graduating from high school or college, getting married, launching a career, having children, retiring. Each passage represents a change in direction, an opportunity to grow, to think in new ways and expand our lives.

No matter where we stand in the arc of experience, we can challenge ourselves to move beyond our own place to empathize with others. Helping our parents and grandparents to navigate safely through their end-of-life passages will profoundly enrich our own journeys through life. Informed by the ever-transforming bond between parent and child, our awareness of the lifepath ripens and matures.

*By honoring our parents' passage, we shape our own,
opening ourselves to a deeper understanding of the world.*

A NEW HOME

*Would the full moon throw a shadow over
the gravel of the drive that was like me?*

ISAK DINESEN

When we feel we belong to a place, perhaps that feeling is a part of knowing ourselves. Unpacking Mom's new apartment at the retirement community—an "independent living unit," to use the lingo—I reassembled the details of her life, box by box, until the rooms took on familiar colors and textures, until the smell of the furniture, curtains, and clothes began to work their way into the walls of the new place. I did it as much for myself as for her. Each object unwrapped and placed "just so" connected us to our family, a life lived and a journey shared. We began to relax, to feel comfortable. Our things remind us of the joy and pain of our lives; help us to recall our place in the world, our bond to the people we love. They are the signposts of our soul.

We can draw strength from this accumulated knowledge of who we are and where we have been, as we start with confidence down a new path. Perhaps, we realize, our center, our *home*, does not truly reside in the treasured objects that travel with us, but in our heart's knowledge of ourselves and in our love for each other.

This is my house and I am still myself.

PROGRESS

———

Success. Four flights Thursday morning.
All against twenty-one-mile wind. Started from level with
engine power alone. Average speed through air thirty-one miles.
Longest fifty-nine seconds.
Inform press. Home Christmas.

WILBUR AND ORVILLE WRIGHT,
TELEGRAM FROM KITTY HAWK, DECEMBER 3, 1903

We live on the edge of a new century. Discoveries are taking place today that will have as profound and dramatic an effect on our lives as this telegram from 1903, announcing the success of air travel. In the 1990s, when flying anywhere on the globe or even into space is no longer thought of as a miracle but as an everyday reality, we can only imagine the world our children and our children's children will navigate in the twenty-first century.

In this fast-paced and transforming time, it is important to remember that ours is not the only enterprising spirit. We build on the successes of the generations before us, so that we might contribute to the successes of the generations that follow us. Consider asking elders in your community to visit your children's schools and speak about the progress gained in their lifetimes. Encourage your children to read biographies and become inspired by the thousands of Americans who have contributed something remarkable to our present—and to their future.

Embrace the enterprising flight of human endeavor.

COOKING SCHOOL

*My Mama! . . . How wonderful the flavor, the aroma of her
kitchen, her stories as she prepared the meal, her Christmas Rolls!
I don't know why mine never turned out like hers, or why my tears
flow so freely when I prepare them—perhaps I am as sensitive
to onions as Tita, my great-aunt, who will go on living
as long as there is someone who cooks her recipes.*

LAURA ESQUIVEL, *LIKE WATER FOR CHOCOLATE*

Jessie, my eighty-eight-year-old Italian grandmother, is teaching me how to roll homemade spaghetti by hand. With great labor and a slowness I don't remember from childhood, she works the dough deftly between her fingers, rolling out the lines of pasta on her own mother's cutting-board, moving to a rhythm generations old, one that has left a deep indentation at the board's center. I watch. I learn.

We cherish the recipes we pass down through families because they possess a flavor and aroma that evokes family members we love. Sometimes the nourishing food connects us to a foreign, distant place where our relatives lived long before coming to this country. We are reminded of the proud and diverse heritage we share as a nation, of our ancestors' courage and determination.

We need to take the time to taste our family's traditions, to savor the skill and talent of its members, passed along to our hands. "Your turn," Gram says, and looks to me.

Learn your family's recipes. Teach them to your children.

READING THE SIGNS

He did not like illness, he distrusted it,
as he distrusted the road without signposts.

EUDORA WELTY

The health problems of elders are often difficult for physicians to diagnose. Symptoms can simply be the common aches and pains of the aging process, or they can signal something deeper and more serious. Elders often have complex combinations of symptoms—chronic back pain, fatigue, or shortness of breath, to name a few, as well as several diagnosed conditions or illnesses. My eighty-eight-year-old grandmother has arthritis, angina pectoris, a hiatal hernia, slipped disk, and high blood pressure!

So, when an aging parent or grandparent doesn't feel well, the answers and solutions may not be obvious ones. This can be alternately frightening or annoying to an older person who wants to know what an ache or pain *really* means (and to family members who ride the roller coaster of "Is this serious or not?" along with their loved one). Also, prescribing the right combinations of medications to treat older persons with multiple illnesses and frail bodies is a challenge for physicians. It is important to make sure the older person in your life is cared for by a geriatrician, a physician trained in treating geriatric patients and accurately prescribing medications for their special needs, or by a primary care physician whose practice focuses on older patients.

Reading the signs and symptoms of aging requires care, attention—
and the aid of a skilled interpreter.

TERRIBLE TWOS

*Children are completely egoistic; they feel their needs intensely
and strive ruthlessly to satisfy them.*

SIGMUND FREUD

Have you ever had an argument with a toddler? One of my best friends, Tamara, has a preschool-age daughter; I love listening to the stories she tells about her relationship with Sydney. "There's a moment," Tamara asserts, "when you find yourself—an intelligent, articulate woman—in a battle of wills with a two-year-old over whether they'll agree to wear an outfit that you, in an effort to be the sensitive, empowering parent, allowed them to pick out for themselves in the *first* place!"

It's no secret that sometimes adults can be "worse than children." You may find yourselves at loggerheads with an aging parent or grandparent over the most trivial of matters, with each encounter or conversation becoming increasingly difficult, almost just for the sake of it. Stubbornness can breed stubbornness, leaving you both feeling gridlocked and accomplishing nothing. When this happens, remember how frustrating it is for your loved one to live with a body that no longer does what it is told to do, who may find certain activities of daily living challenging—activities we wouldn't think twice about doing—or who may just be lonely and angry about it. Look to see if there isn't some deeper need or issue underlying the squabbles and try to address it with compassion and care.

We throw tantrums when we feel our basic needs are thwarted.

SACRED FORMULAS FOR LIVING

Om, shanti, shanti, shanti. . . . All is peace, peace, peace. . . .

HINDU MANTRA

I stayed with Mom for her first two weeks at the retirement community. Excited about all of the activities she could participate in—swim aerobics, art history lectures, travel club, Friday night social—Mom was still anxious about getting around. People who experience the mild dementia of Parkinson's or early Alzheimer's depend upon trusted objects, familiar signposts, and daily routines to know themselves when everything else begins to fall away. I became Mom's guide and confidence booster: Tracing and retracing our steps, I spoke softly to Mom, repeating the name of the complex she lived in, "Herbert's Run," her new phone number, the names of the staff and of other residents we'd meet, hoping the words would sink through her confusion like a life-affirming mantra.

I knew I couldn't be there for Mom this way forever; I felt concerned about her alone in this place, with just enough of her self remaining to comfort her into feeling at home and then betray her in unfamiliar territory. And I told her so. Mom smiled at me in the way a parent smiles at a child who's said something the child thinks is very serious indeed. "We can always hang a sign around my neck with your phone number on it," she suggested. "Relax. You've helped me get started, now I need to find my own way for as long as I can . . . and, by the way, when did you say you'd be back?"

We must all find our own formula for living,
even if we do get some help along the way.

VALUE AGE

. . . I could not, at any age, be content to take my place in a corner
by the fireside and simply look on. Life was meant to be lived.
Curiosity must be kept alive. The fatal thing is the rejection.
One must never, for whatever reason, turn his back on life.

ELEANOR ROOSEVELT

We live in a society that values youth and strength over age and experience. The American Psychiatric Association estimates that nearly one-fourth of people over sixty-five suffer from clinical depression. Increasingly, our elders are beginning to believe that life holds only the grief of loneliness, the despair of restricted movement, illness, and chronic pain. Many turn to thoughts of death as the only viable alternative. What a tragic waste for all of us!

We must encourage our parents and grandparents to value their lives. We must believe that, even now, they can teach us. Remember, these are the people who met the challenge of the Great Depression, fought in World War II and then Korea, and brought about a vast technological revolution that made computers and the information superhighway *possible*.

Our elders are vital, talented people. Spark their interest by involving them in today's challenges.

Our shared curiosity makes wonderful things happen.

WALKING

The swiftest traveler is he that goes afoot.

HENRY DAVID THOREAU

Walking—*ambulating* is the term you might hear physicians use—is an activity that promotes and sustains the basic health of the body. A thirty-minute walk each day keeps muscles toned, aids circulation, stimulates the body's immune system, builds lung capacity, and strengthens cardiovascular health. Not to mention the pleasure gained from getting outdoors and enjoying the local scenery. Taking time out each day for a walk—a good idea for both you *and* your aging parent or grandparent—can help reduce stress, center the mind and body, and allow space for a solitary retreat or an opportunity to enjoy conversation with a walking companion or the people met in the course of a daily ramble. Moving makes us feel engaged in life, a part of the world's continuous motion. If someone you love has restrictions in movement that make long walks difficult, suggest a series of short ten-minute walks—even one five-minute walk can be beneficial. If you can't get outside, walk around the house or even around the room. Of course, always check with your loved one's physician about undertaking any exercise program—even walking—to make sure your walks are consistent with the physician's treatment plan. That done, go for a stroll with your loved one and put your best feet forward!

Celebrate the body in motion. Take a walk and explore your world.

RIGHT BACK HOME

A house can have integrity, just like a person.

AYN RAND

For most of the afternoon, Mom and I practiced finding her apartment at the retirement community, walking scores of times from the elevator bank and using the key to unlock the door. After a while, I stayed by the elevators and watched Mom try it by herself. Things were going poorly. Mom seemed lost; she couldn't get her bearings. Mom's friend Nancy arrived and offered to take over so I could use the time to run some errands. "Okay, Gloria," she said, "we're going to do this." I wandered down the hall behind them as Mom considered door after door, finally settling, by consensus, on her own. She thought she recognized the dried flower wreath on the door. The key would not go in. "This damn key," Mom said. "They'll have to give me a new one." About to step in, I watched as Nancy covered Mom's hand with hers. "Now, Gloria. I *left* my home," she counseled, turning Mom's wrist to the left, "I'm *right* back home. Look."

"Wait a minute," Mom said, and their heads bent close to consider the key and keyhole. "*Right* back home?" I took a step away. "That's right; *right* back home." Right back home.

Finding home is a return to dignity.

28

PATHWAYS

If the path has a heart, then keep walking. . . .

NATIVE AMERICAN SAYING

Ileft my mother's path; it was what we both wanted. Her aspirations for me—go to college, have a career—led me down a new road. She sent me to trailblaze a different way of living. Still, I expected that Mom had to know something about where I was headed, that she could anticipate the signposts, the challenges, the dangers, and the joys waiting for me. Somewhere, we both realized my road would turn and twist in ways neither one of us could reckon from where we stood at the beginning. Perhaps this is true for every generation of mothers and daughters—indeed, of parents and children. What a moment in life when we realize that our paths cannot be precisely plotted! It is both frightening and exhilarating. All we can do is give comfort and encourage one another to go further, discover more.

Now, my mother and I struggle with the path that *she* must take. Neither of us could reckon this turn of events from where we stood at the beginning. Every child who cares for an infirm parent understands the grief over the road that cannot be taken. We share with our parent a sense of disbelief. *Why do we have to walk* this *road?* All we can do is all we have ever been able to do for each other, to give comfort and encouragement and to nurture the heart along its way.

Every path, even the most difficult, contains a heart within.
With love, we can find our way.

WALK-THROUGH

But everybody needs a home so at least you can have something to leave
which is where most other folks will say you must be coming from.

JUNE JORDAN

There is a pride of place that builds with experience and familiarity. Most people hate the idea of change, but more than that, they will balk at the suggestion that it is time to leave a place they call home. My grandmother's geriatrician told me after her most recent checkup that the most therapeutic action she could take would be to move from her home to an apartment or retirement community where she would be less isolated and have more social interaction. My brother and I see the value of this idea, but Jessie won't even consider moving. My mother held onto the family home until the last possible moment. But it is not only our parents and grandparents who can be resistant. It can be hard for us, their children, to think of our parents leaving a family home as well. Our family homes are landmarks that generate a powerful influence in our lives.

On the final walk-through of Mom's house on Kirkwood Road with the real estate broker and the house's new owner—Mom refused to come; she didn't want to see the house without furniture—the emotion of leave-taking flooded my senses. How can empty rooms hold so much? How long will Mom and Mike and Jessie and I walk through these rooms in our minds and in our hearts?

The power of place goes beyond four walls straight to our souls.

GIVE THANKS

—

. . . with countless gifts of love . . .

HYMN

It is a good, uplifting act to give thanks for our lives. Whether we are Christian, Muslim, Buddhist, Jewish, Native American—whatever religion, deeply personal and individual, that we practice—we must not be afraid to rely on the strength of our faith and to share it within our communities.

Most every Sunday I go to Mass. Not just because I believe, but for other reasons, too. For centuries, people have prayed and hoped and dared to believe—in themselves, and in something greater—in holy places like this one. As I stand to profess my faith, I remember standing with my parents, one on either side, resting our hands on the pew in front of us, their grown-up hands covering my small, childish ones. I am here, now, as the representation in flesh and blood of generations of my family—past and future—praying, hoping, daring to believe. At the end of the Mass, the community sings, *Now thank we all our God, with hearts, and hands, and voices.*

When caring for an aging or infirm parent,
let your faith stand strong in the comfort
and celebration of living.

MOVING IN

Home is the place where, when you have to go there,
They have to take you in.

ROBERT FROST

A room isn't a house," Gram Granger said when she moved into my brother's old room after surgery for colon cancer at age seventy-six. Mom's mom was a fiercely independent person. Sylvia is gone several years now; she lived in my mother's house on Kirkwood Road for the last year of her life. But she never sold her own house; my uncle took care of keeping it up for her and Sylvia always believed she'd be going back into her own home eventually.

When the best choice for care is to have your parent or grandparent move in with you, temporarily or permanently, remember that it is often as hard for them to come as it is for you—juggling careers, kids, a house, and a spouse—to take them in; more than one lifestyle and set of habits will have to adjust to change. If you are open-minded, you may discover that even as you are opening your home with generosity, you are on the receiving end as well, and I mean this in a good way! Instead of a grudging burden or a nagging imposition, make your aging parent feel a welcome addition to the household: a contributing member of the family. I wouldn't trade memories of visits to Baltimore that last summer, playing Scrabble with Mom and Gram Granger, drinking iced tea under the porch awning. Sylvia could take forty-five minutes to play a word. I'd tell her, "While we're young, Gram. While we're young."

Draw strength from your family as it draws strength from you.

THE BODY IN TIME

Age will not be defied.

FRANCIS BACON

As the body ages, several factors conspire to make getting around more difficult. The lungs become less elastic, the heart less efficient; muscles and bones lose strength and mass; pressure on disks causes wear on the hip and knee joints; arteries harden, causing poor circulation and an increase in blood pressure; the liver is less effective in processing body toxins; and the loss of nerve cells slows reaction times and renders the senses less acute. According to the American Medical Association, eighty-five—the age designated for the "oldest old"—is the average age to which the human body can aspire without the intrusion of illness and disease.

It's hard to accept the fact that our bodies age according to biological processes we cannot alter or reverse (though medical technology and the cosmetics industry keep trying!). We need to realize that the human body makes passages, has "seasons," just as surely as the human spirit and understanding progress, evolving over a lifetime. Perhaps, instead of imposing on age an impossible ideal of youthful physical strength, we should embrace the aging body for the power inherent in the maturity and spiritual prowess of its glorious winter. I have two photographs of Jessie, my father's mother, portraits framed sided by side: one at thirty when she, a determined Italian immigrant, became a U.S. citizen; the other on the day she reached her eighty-fifth year of life. Both faces are beautiful.

An old face accumulates the textures of experience.

33

RECORD KEEPING

There is something about a bureaucrat that does not like a poem.

GORE VIDAL

Getting and keeping copies of medical records, such as laboratory reports, X-ray or mammogram films, or written summaries of treatments suggested or provided by consulting specialists (a radiologist, gynecologist, or cardiologist, for example), is essential to building a complete personal health profile that may prove invaluable for receiving the best and most accurate health care. Upon request, most pharmacists can also generate a computer printout of all prescriptions for medications filled during any calendar year. This list is a good record not only of the names of medications taken, but of the specific dosages prescribed and the length of time your parent or grandparent has been taking each drug.

This records profile can be especially helpful for an aging person who may be undergoing treatment for multiple health problems or conditions and who may be taking a combination of prescribed and over-the-counter medications; physicians will want to know what treatments or therapies are currently being received or have been received in the past.

Be assertive: All individuals have the legal right to request and receive a copy or summary of their own personal medical records. A recent Tufts University study reveals that patients whose physicians show them their medical records and provide strategies for treatment are in better health than those patients who do not view their records and discuss treatment alternatives.

Have your aging parent or grandparent regularly request copies of medical records at each visit with a physician. Or draft a letter to the physician for your loved one to sign requesting that records be routinely provided; this letter itself will become a part of the permanent medical record. If you possess an active durable power of attorney for health care for your loved one, health care professionals must release records to you as your loved one's legal agent and provide you full access to their medical charts and files.

Take action for better health: Get and keep medical records.

DRIVING

Any color—so long as it's black.

HENRY FORD, ON THE MODEL T

My mother wouldn't give up the car. Cars are such a symbol of independence, freedom, and status in American life. Not driving a car is like being a dependent child. But things were going wrong. Minor events: turning without signaling, fender benders in parking lots, getting lost, going the wrong way on one-way streets. Minor events that could have a major impact, causing damage to property or, worse, to life—her own or someone else's. Mom waved it off; "I'll only drive in a five-mile radius from home," she said. "What can happen?"

"No," I said, giving my mother an ultimatum for the first time in my life. "You can't take the chance anymore. Ask any one of your friends. Ask your doctors. They'll all tell you the same thing. Driving is too dangerous now." After much arguing and hashing about, we agreed that Mom would keep her car so that her friends could use it to go places with her, but that she would not drive it herself until her physician confirmed that driving was once again safe. The solution gave Mom a way to hold onto a degree of independence. For as long as she had the car, Mom used the threat of driving to bust through any roadblock she felt contributed to a loss of her control over her own life. "I'll just get in the car and drive," she'd say. It was a sign to me that some other issue needed to be addressed with care.

We may give up the driver's seat,
but we still want to chart our own courses.

COURAGE

Courage is as often the outcome of despair as of hope; in the one case we have nothing to lose, in the other everything to gain.

DIANE DE POITIERS

I am always worried about my mother. What does she need? Is she happy? Is she comfortable? Is she in pain? What can I do? *I am my mother's mother now*, I think to myself. Sometimes, in moments of confusion, she even calls me "Mom." Yet that's not right; I am not her parent.

We all look to our parents, no matter what our age or theirs, as a source of strength. Well, it is one thing to find out that our parents are human, that they have limits. But when the roles reverse, we can be shocked to discover that our parents need us to help and guide them. The childlike status of our own mother or father is a painful discovery that can lead us to feel abandoned and parentless at the very moment we are supplying them with comfort and care.

I understand that I will always be my mother's child. I also understand that she can no longer protect me. And that is when I need my courage the most. Courage comes from the grief that pushes us to take charge of our own lives, even as our parents lose the ability to take charge of theirs. Courage also comes with the willingness to be truthful about the situation, to really *be* someone's child, experiencing and learning from every growing pain as we care for our aging parents.

"Child" and "parent" can be more than one-note stereotypes.
Find the courage to grow with the roles.

FAILURE

If you have made mistakes, even serious ones,
there is always another chance for you. What we call failure is
not the falling down, but the staying down.

MARY PICKFORD

Sometimes we fail. Instead of being one step ahead we feel lucky if we're only one step behind. Voice after voice calls out a new responsibility: coworkers, kids, spouse, friends, parents—until the only answer we want to give is, *Leave me alone!*

We're only individuals. Even if for a short time we can pull off doing everything for everybody, at some point we burn out and something falls through the cracks, gets lost, is left undone, or gets broken. When this happens, we feel the weight of our responsibilities drag us down.

Yes, sometimes we fail. Yes, there are times when we are better employees, parents, spouses, and caregivers to our aging parents. We won't always know the right thing to do or make the best choices every time. But we keep going—doing the best we can one day at a time, one step at a time.

Instead of seeing only what's gone wrong,
focus on the love and determination that keeps us moving.

PILLBOX

Seniors often take several different kinds of medication, each with their own prescribed dosages and administration times. It can be a challenge for *anyone,* young or old, to keep it all straight, and especially so for an older person who may be experiencing the confusion and disorientation of mild dementia. Sometimes, an older person might insist that he or she is taking medication properly when you know that just isn't the case. Either the drug therapy seems not to be working, or the prescription just isn't being used up in the proper amount of time, or side effects from taking too much or too little of the drug become apparent.

It is essential that seniors take their medications exactly as the physician has prescribed. One effective solution is to find the right pillbox. You can buy boxes that have separate compartments for each day of the week, or are numbered by dose. Some boxes have large printing for older people who have trouble reading. In every case, you'll want to look for a box that is easy to open, particularly for someone with arthritis. You can also make your own. Save an empty egg carton and use a marker to label each "egg" with the dose to be taken. Color-code the carton, if colors are easier for your loved one to identify than words. Pillboxes also help make seniors "accountable" for remembering to take their medications. If they don't take them, well, *Who are you gonna believe . . . ?*

Take as directed *can mean the difference between health and illness.*

CATARACTS

Things don't change. You change your way of looking, that's all.

CARLOS CASTANEDA

My eighty-eight-year-old grandmother never had any kind of surgery—that is, until one of her cataracts was removed two years ago. Getting her to have that cataract removed required a gargantuan (yes, that's the only word to describe it) effort of persuasion from my brother, Mike, and me and Gram's doctors. Jessie was skeptical about just how "easy" the procedure would be. She threw up every obstacle she could think of, cantankerous with fear.

The promise of modern medicine held no allure for Jessie. In Gram's mind, hospitals loomed as a risky haven at best. When she was a young woman, most people couldn't afford the hospital and didn't even have insurance; you went to the hospital when you were so sick you didn't have any other choice. Hospitals were places best avoided. Almost blind, though, even Jessie knew that if she wanted to remain independent, she had to give in sooner than later. The tactic that finally worked: I told Gram I'd go with her on a plane trip to California to visit Mike—but only if she could *see*.

"Nothing to it," she told us after the surgery. Meanwhile, she'd told her entire life story to the nurses and gotten them all to promise to come and visit her at home. Most people over sixty-five have some cataract development and by age seventy-five are experiencing some loss of vision. Cataract removal is a procedure tailor-made for the elderly and is so commonly performed it is viewed by physicians as almost routine. The benefits to a senior's quality of daily living far outweigh the risks of the procedure, which, according to the American Medical Association, is one of the least complex and most successful operations performed. (Now, Gram, about that other cataract. California beckons. . . .)

The soul peers through cataracts as through a misty waterfall, descending. Restore a clear, unobstructed view.

A LITTLE DINNER CONVERSATION

Life loves to be taken by the lapel and told:
"I am with you kid. Let's go."

MAYA ANGELOU

Mom and I are waiting to be called for dinner in the retirement community's dining hall. Just as at a restaurant, we give our names and wait in the lounge near the fireplace for our turn to be seated. "Chearney, party of two," the hostess announces, and we are seated at a table with three lovely ladies. Dinner at the retirement community is quite a social event. This apartment complex and dining hall have only recently opened, so everyone is new here, making introductions and getting oriented. "Have you been to the pool yet?" one woman asks. "I took the shuttle bus to the chapel yesterday," another comments. Mom laments that she is having trouble figuring out how to find her apartment and all three of our dinner mates nod their heads empathetically. "Give yourself a couple of days," they say.

By the end of the meal these women have forged a bond. Mom, who seemed so grateful for my presence only an hour before, seems ready to shed me as eagerly as I shed her when I was a teenager going out for fun with a bunch of friends from school. "Gloria, there's a movie tonight. Do you want to go? Let's all go." Four heads turn my way.

"Okay, Mom," I say. "But be home before midnight—and make sure someone sees you to the door."

Welcome good times with new friends.

ACT YOUR AGE

It was wonderful. I'm a new man.

FORMER U.S. PRESIDENT GEORGE BUSH,
AFTER PARACHUTING OVER THE ARIZONA DESERT AT AGE SEVENTY-TWO

The average life expectancy in 1900 was about forty-five years; today, it's around seventy-five. In 1944 during World War II—the last time George Bush parachuted out of a plane, jumping into the Pacific Ocean after his bomber was shot down by the Japanese—only eight percent of the world's population was over age sixty-five. By the year 2050 there could be as many as 100 million people over the age of sixty-five. Just what does being "old" mean? For our parents' generation, it can mean something new, vital, and exciting.

The negative stereotypes about aging are challenged every day by over-sixty-fivers who lead active, vibrant lives. Just because someone is over sixty-five doesn't mean we—or they—should assume pursuing a full life is inappropriate or impossible. So, when your parents or grandparents want to take that trip to Las Vegas, learn to play the piano, play sports, take a college course, or cruise the Antarctic, cheer them on.

And if your parents or grandparents are stuck in the belief that old age is empty and purposeless, tell them they are wrong.

In the twenty-first century, being old will have a new meaning, a meaning pioneered by today's seniors. Aging is an opportunity to meld vitality with the maturity experience brings.

COMPASSION

What value has compassion that does not take its object in its arms?

ANTOINE DE SAINT-EXUPÉRY

My brother, Mike, and my parents have had a difficult relationship—and that is a kind way to put it—for as long as I can remember. Mike is seven years older than I am. When I was in high school, Mike told our parents he was gay. They reacted with anger and a disbelief that deepened into something worse than denial; they chose to ignore it. When pushed, my parents accepted any reminder of the truth as if it were a personal affront or an insult—as if my brother were gay simply to hurt or embarrass them. My parents' lack of compassion hurt Mike and our whole family. Loving them all, I felt torn apart and angry in the midst of a family where proving love for one person meant accepting or rejecting someone else.

When a parent becomes ill and needs help, difficult relationships do not resolve by magic. Age and infirmity do not erase problems between people. The old hurts remain, and there are no easy answers or quick fixes. Expect emotions to run high. Strive to understand and respect how each family member feels, to see things from each unique perspective. Mending family relationships requires empathy, honesty, and a *mutual* willingness to open minds, hearts, and hands to embrace each other, maybe for the first time in our lives.

To be forgiven, we must first be able to forgive.

BOUQUET

Imagine killing all those young flowers for the sake of an old woman.

COLETTE

What do you get for someone who has everything? Or who says they don't want anything? Flowers! Some older people love receiving floral arrangements on special occasions or as a reminder that you are thinking of them. Some things to consider when sending flowers to older friends or relatives:

✵ What kinds of flowers does the older person like? (As opposed to what *you* like . . .)

✵ Does the person have respiratory problems, asthma, or allergies that might make flowers a bad choice?

✵ Does the older person have a garden or lots of house-plants? Something that can be repotted or planted might be appreciated more than cut flowers.

✵ Has the older person recently had eye surgery (cataract surgery, for instance) or have eye problems? Flowers and plants can carry germs from the hands to the eyes and may not be advisable or allowed. Ask before sending an arrangement.

✵ Balloons! Singing telegrams! (Enough said.)

✲ How well does the older person see? Someone who can't see very well may not get much out of flowers. If a person with impaired vision really loves flowers, though, choose varieties that are fragrant or rich in texture.

✲ Consider a "flowers all year round" plan. Florists can deliver different varieties each month. Your loved one might consider the attention flattering and the flowers a bright pleasure to look forward to.

A little thought can make a routine gesture
an intimate, loving action.

FIGURES

Money, which represents the prose of life,
and which is hardly spoken of in parlors without an apology, is,
in its effects and laws, as beautiful as roses.

RALPH WALDO EMERSON

Mom could no longer keep her money straight. A woman who had never used a calculator, who had added long columns of numbers in her head with speed, now fumbled with the simplest figures. Mom's closest friends, Nancy and Miss Jean, would help Mom to balance her checkbook, but that could only go on for so long. Finally, Mom couldn't hide the disorganized state of her financial affairs from me any longer. We were all afraid that Mom would be taken advantage of by unscrupulous strangers or that she would pay her bills incorrectly or not at all.

Still, Mom rankled over giving up control over her money. Her reaction to my suggestion that I manage her checkbook was mixed with fear, distrust, and anger: fear that if she delegated the paying of bills to me, I might forget something or do something wrong; distrust—not of me, of course, but what if I started going out with a man who might sway my better judgment and leave us both vulnerable to his questionable influence, swindled (Thanks, Mom!); anger that her child wanted to "take her money away from her."

So, instead we tried starting with a calculator with large buttons and a big display screen and practiced with that. But it didn't work. Mom just didn't like calculators—she didn't trust the math and would still try to add the figures herself. The checkbook was a mess again.

Next, Mom started saving all the bills and we would do the finances together once a month. The trouble with this was that Mom continued to use the checkbook during the month and I could never be sure her balance was right until I checked it against the bank statement.

Finally, Mom agreed to open two checking accounts: one with a preset balance of $250 that she could use as she pleased, and the main account that I would use to pay her regular bills directly. We had her pension and Social Security checks direct-deposited into the main account so there would be fewer trips to the bank. We got one all-purpose credit card for Mom to use while shopping so she wouldn't have to handle money or write checks. Through it all, I reassured Mom that I was simply her bookkeeper. I made no comments about where and how Mom spent her money unless she asked my opinion or the sum was large enough to have an impact on the big financial picture and I wanted to be sure that Mom understood the effect the expense would have.

Each month I reported to Mom that the bills had been paid and went through the list with her to make sure everything had been taken care of. I balanced her "spending money" checkbook against the statement and made a deposit to bring the balance back up to $250. Mom never really liked this arrangement, but she came to accept it. It was better than all the trouble she'd been having, and she became grudgingly convinced that she still retained the freedom to spend what she wanted, when and how she liked.

Managing money requires an elaborate negotiation of commerce and trust.

AT THE OLD TOWN

To be wildly enthusiastic, or deadly serious—both are wrong.
Both pass. One must keep ever present a sense of humor.

KATHERINE MANSFIELD

Sitting in the Old Town, a landmark New York tavern, I am having a beer with my friend David Gorman. I had just gotten back from a long week taking care of Mom in Baltimore and I was tired. "Don't you wish," I said to David, "that just for five minutes, your father was alive so you could ask him questions, find out why things are the way they are, have a shoulder to rest your *own* shoulder on for a change? What would you say to him?"

"My father?" David asked. "I'd say, 'You're dead. What are you doing here?'" And we both burst out laughing. When you think about it, we probably believe our parents have access to more of the answers we are searching for than they likely would, or that they'd be able to help us when, in truth, we'll never have the opportunity to see how our deceased parents may have handled the illness or infirmity of their spouses. We're left to our own resources, with a lot of unknowables attached. But I did find one important answer at the Old Town with David: Laughter helps you keep your perspective better than just about anything.

Cultivating a healthy sense of humor helps us cope with the strong
emotions that come with stressful situations.

RESEARCH

Research is formalized curiosity. It is poking and prying with a purpose.

Zora Neale Hurston

There are so many ways to access information these days: books, newspapers, magazines, newsletters, and journals; investigative reports and documentaries on television; local and national organizations and associations; archives; government agencies; on-line resources, such as Web sites and databases on the Internet; information brokers; CD-ROMs, audiotapes, and videos. There's so much information that it is easy to feel inundated and overwhelmed. And many times we come up with conflicting data and/or disagreeing points of view.

How can we decide what information is reliable and trustworthy when we are researching issues related to the health and care of our aging parents and grandparents? Try not to let the plethora of information choices discourage your impulse to *do* research. When in doubt, take your research findings to the appropriate expert who can help you analyze and assess your options. Then, after carefully weighing the issues at hand, make your own informed decisions.

Never before have ordinary citizens had the power to access such a great wealth of knowledge, becoming better equipped than at any time in history to use cutting-edge, state-of-the-art breakthroughs to enhance their own lives. Instead of being intimidated by the information superhighway, jump on. Ask your local librarian to help you find the on-ramp. There are good answers to your questions.

Gather information: Call your own meeting of the experts.

MOVING ON

One can never consent to creep when one feels an impulse to soar.

HELEN KELLER

For seniors who have difficulty walking and getting around, there are a number of assistive devices that can keep them safely mobile. A geriatrician and/or physical therapist can help you choose, measure, and fit the device that best suits your loved one's physical condition and provide instruction in its proper use. Assistive devices consist of a variety of canes, crutches, and walkers.

Standard canes are useful for people who have weakness or pain only on one side or who need minor help in balancing. A quad cane, or a standard cane on a four-legged base, provides more stability but still requires the user to have upper body strength and balance control. A very sturdy cane is the walk-cane, which has four legs and a handlebar seniors can hold onto. Walkcanes are excellent for people who have suffered cerebrovascular accidents (CVAs), or strokes, and who may be experiencing hemiplegia, or paralysis on one side of the body.

Platform crutches, where the user rests the weight of the forearm on a platform that sits atop the crutch, is a good alternative for arthritic users who cannot grip or bear weight with the hands and works better than a cane. Axillary crutches, the kind that fit under the armpits, are dangerous for older people and should be avoided as a walking aid; these crutches require dexterity and strength.

Walkers, which come with and without wheels, are wonderful for older people, giving the best stability and support. Rolling walkers are advantageous particularly for people who require more help with balance than support. Walkers have one more plus: Seniors can attach a carry bag or tote to the front of the walker for transporting small, lightweight objects. For travel away from home, however, such as a shopping trip or family visit, it is advisable to keep a wheelchair handy for a senior's maximum comfort and to avoid fatigue.

Wings come in all shapes and sizes.

IN THE WOMEN'S ROOM

. . . as awareness increases, the need for personal secrecy
almost proportionately decreases.

CHARLOTTE PAINTER

Urinary incontinence is one of those subjects—like menstruation, labor pains, and menopause—women traditionally never discussed, not even with each other. Today, all that is changing. But for older women, like my eighty-eight-year-old grandmother, times may change but viewpoints don't.

Indeed, Jessie confided in me only because I discreetly made it clear that I knew what was going on; she couldn't hide her situation. A lot of older women remain housebound and silent, withdrawn and embarrassed, rather than admit they are having trouble controlling their urination. If they do leave the house, it's only for an hour or two and then straight back home again. Appallingly, some older women refuse to drink a lot of fluids so they won't urinate as much. We need to remind them that staying hydrated is by far the more important goal.

Fortunately, urinary incontinence can be lessened and sometimes eliminated. Foremost, discuss the problem candidly with a geriatrician or urologist to determine treatment options. Encourage your loved one to try out the many varieties of pads available. Plan outings wisely—build in time for regular trips to accessible bathrooms, use a wheelchair or limit time walking so that vaginal and pelvic muscles don't get overly fatigued, and always exhibit sensitivity and patience.

Secrecy and discretion are two different concepts!
Secrecy hides passively while discretion acts with good judgment.

CABLE GAL

Just recently I ordered cable for my grandmother. "It's great," I said. "You never get out of the house anymore. TV is a way you can stay connected with the world. You'll have a channel for news, a channel for weather, a channel that shows old movies all day. You'll love it."

"Don't get that for me," Jessie says. "I don't want it." Too bad. After a day or so of exciting visits from the cable guy, my grandmother was wired. It lasted a week. "It's confusing. I can't find the channels I like." All the cliches about older people and "modern conveniences" can be true. Some take: The bread machine was a big hit (even though it's not the same as kneading your own), so was the telephone with the big numbers on it and caller ID (you can never be too careful ...). Some don't take: VCRs, cable, and most electronic devices are shunned. Still, you've got to try. "And those *computers* ..." my grandmother complains. "Every time I use the telephone it's press *this* number or press *that* number. And when you do, you never get the right person. It's all so screwy. I tell them all to go to hell." I know what you mean, Gramma.

When cutting-edge products and technologies are modern "inconveniences" to an older person, don't force a square peg into a round hole. Then again, rejoice when you find a perfect fit.

PANTY HOSE

Everything is funny so long as it is happening to someone else.

WILL ROGERS

For as long as she could, my mother remained determined to dress herself. My grandmother, Jessie, is just as stubborn about it to this day. They are both women who like clothes and like looking good. Panty hose, of course, are a wardrobe staple. Gloria could struggle upwards of an hour putting on panty hose, talking to herself through every minute of it. And my grandmother only recently capitulated to the dreaded "thigh high" alternative.

I remember one episode when I decided to intervene. As I walked into Mom's bedroom, she stood in front of the bureau mirror, lipstick in hand, close to tears. The panty hose were twisted, inside out, one leg on, one leg off. Clothes were strewn across the bed. She'd given up and switched to applying makeup with shaky hands. "Just look at me," she said. I knew it was a crucial moment.

"No problem, Mom, you should see me get dressed. It takes me an hour just to decide what to wear." We started with the panty hose. It became kind of like playing a game of Twister and before we knew it we were both hysterical laughing and crying.

"Some man must have invented these in the middle ages to keep women from ever going out of the house," Mom said. You've got to laugh about it. Shortly thereafter, Mom switched from skirts, hose, and heels to pants, socks, and flats. She could be comfortable and still look great.

Beauty, style, and grace aren't about what *we wear, but* how *we wear it.*

SIMPLE JOYS

"When you wake up in the morning, Pooh," said Piglet at last,
"what's the first thing you say to yourself?"
"What's for breakfast?" said Pooh. "What do you say, Piglet?"
"I say, I wonder what's going to happen exciting today?"said Piglet.

A. A. MILNE

Excitement can be found in the daily ritual joys of meal-times, an afternoon walk, or the evening paper. It can be found in new friends made as well as old ones remembered. It can rest in a kind offer of help from a neighbor. In the upturned smiles of our children and grandchildren. Perhaps, if we believe that each day holds the promise of captivating and delighting us, even the pureness of a deep breath of morning air—one that fills our lungs to the deepest point—can remind us we are alive and ready to share the miracle of our experiences with others.

We need to embrace where we are in the journey of life. When we care for an aging parent or grandparent, we can encourage them, as they encourage us, to enjoy every moment of living. Every moment of living, something *happens!*

With the innocent joy of a child,
look for the excitement that lives in each moment.

HOUSEGUEST

Some people can stay longer in an hour than others can in a week.

WILLIAM DEAN HOWELLS

When children live in a different city or state from their aging parents, sooner or later one or the other is bound to become a houseguest. Ideal houseguests are people who enjoy entering their host's environment and who look forward to participating, respectfully, in the routines and patterns of the household. Well, that's the ideal houseguest. The problem with intergenerational visits is that the host and guest are invariably in different times of life, with different habits, interests, and levels of energy. Compromise is necessary for host and guest to collaborate on a successful visit.

I have one friend, Bruce, who struggled with the fact that his mother would come up for a summer week to enjoy the beautiful Hudson Valley of New York with him and his wife, Kathy, and then never want to leave the house. In a recent visit to his mother's condo in Florida, Bruce and Kathy saw the relief on his mom's face when he suggested they just hang out and go to the movies with her and her friends instead of trying to sightsee. Some other friends, who have small children, were upset when their parents booked a hotel room rather than stay with them—until they realized it was a matter of energy, not love. One or two hours with the kids was about all their parents could handle without becoming exhausted.

When she could, my mom used to come to New York from Baltimore and spend as much as a month at a time—a feat of accommodation we *both* found to be a tall order. But how I'd love it if I could spend time shopping at Macy's, eating out, and seeing Broadway shows with Mom, just once more. . . .

My dear friend Bill Mortimer loves to remember the time he had dinner with Mom and me at a favorite restaurant, long gone now, in Greenwich Village, called Joe's. Mom was still doing fine then. Bill sat across from us at the table and watched the mother-daughter mirror in motion with wry amusement. "You know," he said later, "you're so much . . ."

"Don't say it," I jumped in. "Don't go there!"

"Like her."

A successful visit is one that brings your hearts closer together.

WHAT DID YOU SAY?

If there are any of you at the back who do not hear me,
please don't raise your hands because I am also nearsighted.

W. H. AUDEN

A lot of older people don't like to admit they are losing their hearing—if they even notice it themselves. How many times have you walked into your parent's or grandparent's house to find the TV set blaring? Or how many times has your parent become irritable because people "aren't speaking up"? The cause has always got to be some outside source, not something intimately connected to themselves—like hearing loss.

According to the Mayo Clinic, more than one-third of people over the age of sixty-five experience some level of hearing loss due to the natural process of aging. The medical term for this is *presbycusis*. Elders with hearing loss can behave out of character, becoming more isolated, withdrawn, and timid in social situations where they feel increasingly left out.

If someone you love is having trouble hearing, suggest visiting an audiologist to be tested for a hearing aid. But there are other things you can do to make communication easier for your aging parent or grandparent. When watching TV, turn on the closed-captioning now available on all new TV sets. When conversing together, stay in the same room and eliminate any environmental noises that could distract your loved one. Speak at a slow but natural pace; speaking louder won't improve someone's ability to understand.

Most important, establish eye contact with your parent or grandparent before you start talking and be sure you are not standing in front of a brightly lit window or in a dimly lit area where your face cannot be clearly seen. Use natural gesture to help get your point across.

Whatever you do, keep communicating—that's the most important thing.

Hearing is only one way to receive communication.

ASK YOUR DOCTOR

You know doctors. For every one thing they tell you,
there are two things hidden under the tongue.

ROSE CHERNIN

My mother always hated it when I asked her doctor questions. "The doctor is too busy for this," she'd cut me—and the physician—off. My grandmother, on the other hand, loves it when I ask questions on her behalf. "It is important to know the truth about your health," she says. Personally, I agree with Gram. Indeed, patients' active participation as full members of the health care team is vital to their receipt of timely, successful treatment. People need to view themselves as equal partners in their own care, matching the 100 percent effort from the physicians, nurses, physical therapists, or other health care professionals involved in restoring their health and vitality. Physicians, however, often look for a person's "readiness or willingness to know" and could misgauge reticence or shyness as a desire "not to know more than is absolutely necessary." Physicians may then be less forthcoming with details and extra information about an illness or condition unless the patient actively seeks it out. So, ask about diet; exercise; support groups; the range of traditional treatments or therapies available; the effectiveness of complementary alternative medicine disciplines, such as chiropractic, massage, or acupuncture; possible drug interactions; home health aids—in short, anything and everything you can think of!

Get involved in your own care and treatment:
The health you improve could be your own!

HOLDING ON

*The beauty of the world has two edges, one of laughter,
one of anguish, cutting the heart asunder.*

VIRGINIA WOOLF

During my father's illness fifteen years ago, I remember coming from New York to the house on Kirkwood Road in Baltimore for a long weekend to help my parents out, and finding the tension in the house so thick you could cut it with a knife. Mom and Dad weren't talking, and Mom definitely seemed grateful to use me as a diversion to avoid facing him. My parents were never ones to argue much in front of me, and I felt really uncomfortable. So I went to the video store and rented one of Dad's favorite movies: *The Thomas Crown Affair.* Halfway through, I looked over and saw an expression of sheer despair on my father's face. I went over to him and hugged him; we held on that way for five minutes.

When I went into the kitchen to get Dad a snack, Mom stood in tears trying to prepare dinner. "I can't hug him anymore," she said. "He used to wrap me up in his arms and now . . . I can't bear it, Lee Ann, it breaks my heart." I put my arm around Mom's shoulder.

I understood that day that there was more at stake than just Dad's health. Dad's sense of identity—vital, gregarious, hardworking—was threatened by the cancer. Fragile, my parents struggled to find something familiar to hold onto, something abiding and strong. They looked for it in their lifelines, their children.

Our families hold a circle of growing strength.

AN OUNCE OF PREVENTION

Feel joy. And have a positive attitude toward life.

Dr. Larry Norton, oncologist, Memorial Sloan-Kettering, on being asked what patients can do to help fight cancer

How often do we include "the joy of living" on our list of short- and long-term goals? And, even if we do, is it a real priority? We can lose sight of life's joyfulness when we are overwhelmed with responsibilities, stress, the hundred details of each day's activity. We are so caught up that we forget about what it is we *are* doing: living! In our nation's Declaration of Independence, Thomas Jefferson upheld this truth as self-evident: Every person is "endowed by their creator with certain unalienable rights; that among these are life, liberty, and the pursuit of happiness." As caregivers, we must tend to and nurture a daily observance of these rights both for ourselves and for our aging parents and grandparents.

Whenever we encounter another person, their own love of life, their spirit of joy, radiates from them, reaching out to touch us and affect our lives. Recent medical studies by researchers such as behaviorial scientist Sandra Levy, Ph.D., and epidemiologist Elizabeth Maunsell, Ph.D., reveal that people who show a capacity for joy at the start of their illnesses and people who have strong social support from friends and family also have a higher rate of long-term survival. How wonderful, that our best preventive medicine can be the joy of living itself!

Help your loved ones to connect to their own joy of living.
Enjoy simple pleasures together.

FAMILY LEAVE

Work is love made visible.

KAHLIL GIBRAN

Nearly one-third of all American employees are involved to some extent in the care of an aging parent or relative. The Family and Medical Leave Act, passed in 1993, gives workers the opportunity to take up to twelve weeks of unpaid time off to care for an ill parent—with thirty days' advance notice given, if possible. If you think your situation qualifies for family and medical leave, consult your company's human resources department. Be aware that you can take the leave in small increments—as little as a day, or even a morning or afternoon—if your employer approves.

In our high-pressured, fast-paced work environment, people are often afraid that taking open advantage of family and medical leave time will compromise their reputation as committed employees, endanger the security of their jobs, or cause resentment from coworkers. We need, as citizens, to reinforce that we can be good employees and good family members, too. Working hard and caring for our families are equal pursuits in American life, and we must exercise our right, under the law, to preserve the sanctity of both.

We can take care of business—personal and professional—
with integrity and devotion.

FLU SHOT

Jessie doesn't want to get her flu shot. "Gram," I lecture her, "you have to do this. When you get older, your immune system is not as strong as it used to be and you need to get it."

"It makes me sick." Jessie's eyebrows raise and lower. "That better not be a flu shot," she tells the medical assistant. "My granddaughter told you to give it to me but I don't want it."

The medical assistant pauses, holds the syringe in midair, and looks at me. "You two have to work this out," she says.

I give Gram my father's famous squinty-eyed glare, the one that used to send me running as a child. He got the look from her. Jessie laughs. "I'm telling you," she says, rolling up her sleeve and nodding toward her arm, "flu shots make me sick."

"Old people," I say to the medical assistant who wisely ignores me as she checks one more time to make sure my grandmother acquiesces and professionally administers the injection.

Preventive medicine is worth the effort of persistence and persuasion.

DREAMS

. . . for there comes a time when you have to take your life in your arms.

ANN FARADAY

We all dream. Each night we close our eyes and open our minds to an unconscious world that is the blueprint of our souls. For many weeks I puzzled over a series of dreams about a brunette woman, my age, with whom I argued constantly and who opposed me everywhere. Finally, I had this dream: We are about to get on the Fifth Avenue bus in midtown New York City, right near Rockefeller Center, when I step back. I've had enough of this woman. "I don't want to take that bus. I never take that bus. The subway is faster. You'll have to take that bus alone," I tell her, tired of being forced into doing things her way in these dreams. When she turns around, it is the face of my sixty-five-year-old mother, and she is terrified. "Don't make me go alone," she says as I rocket awake. Mom.

We gain powerful insights by opening our hearts to the messages of our dreams. Our dreams synthesize our unconscious thoughts and feelings, giving them shape and substance. Welcome your dreams, even your nightmares, as your mind's way to move deeper issues into the light of your conscious awareness. Give it a try. Use your dreams to wake you up to your innermost self, the truth of your thoughts, actions, and feelings.

When you go to sleep, ask your dreams to come to you.
Tell them you are ready.

CHOICES

In my life's chain of events nothing was accidental.
Everything happened according to an inner need.

HANNAH SENESH

When I asked my brother, Mike, what he felt was the most important message he could convey to readers of this book, he said, "Everyone is responsible for their own life." Every day all of us make dozens of choices, large and small, immediate and far-reaching. We can choose to take everything upon ourselves, the brave martyr or bully who holds up the world. We can choose to let others take charge, becoming either annoying backseat drivers in our own lives or passive participants in a parade of life that marches on by. We can even choose to give up our own dreams to nuture someone else's—a child's, a spouse's, a parent's. Or, we can choose to turn away and march to our own drummer. We can choose to isolate ourselves, or we can choose to join in. There are as many paths to choose as there are people in the world. But, no matter how we live our lives, as Harry Truman put it, "The buck stops here." Our lives bear the consequences of our own actions and decisions, whether we, or the ones we love, admit it or not. And these consequences will have ramifications everywhere we go, on everything we touch.

We are the authors of our own experience.

LICENSE

I am in the DMV with Mom to renew her driver's license. She hadn't been driving for quite some time, but she just wouldn't, *couldn't*, let that license expire. We argued all the way up to the counter. "Face facts, Mom," I said. "Your doctor says you shouldn't be driving. You don't drive. Maybe it's time to give the car to Uncle Donald and we'll just get a picture ID from the DMV that you can carry for identification." The reply: Absolutely no!

I watched Mom struggle to fill out the renewal form, her writing hand shaky from Parkinson's, but she managed to get through that step. Then, the clerk pointed Mom to the vision test. *Here it comes.* Mom hesitated over the eyepiece, slow in answering the questions the clerk asked her about what she saw. "It's these reading glasses," Mom said. The clerk suggested she take the glasses off. Mom complied. The test began again. Mom seemed confused. "You're nervous," the clerk kindly offered. "Try again." Mom fumbled. Glasses on, glasses off. The clerk looked at me, but I offered no help. That patient clerk gently gave my mother at least five chances to pass. Mom stood determined, crestfallen. Suddenly, I understood how parents feel when their children venture out to master the world. Joy for every success. A broken heart for every setback. We cried together that day.

To grow, sometimes we have to let the ones we love make their own mistakes.

TALKING

I got well by talking. Death could not get a word in edgewise,
grew discouraged, and traveled on.

LOUISE ERDRICH

I've heard my grandmother's stories a million times. I used to wonder whether she knew she was repeating herself, over and over and over, or whether Jessie actually thought she was revealing something new. Eventually, I saw that the answer was a little of both. Now, I listen and wait to discover what variation of a story Gram will tell—some stories have four or five different twists; or I ponder why Gram chooses to tell a certain story at a particular moment—is there some unconscious meaning in the memory? In any case, Gram's stories are precious and vital to her survival. At eighty-eight, Gram uses her stories as one of the only ways left to her through which she can actively connect her past to her present: Most of the people and places in these stories are gone or changed. So it is more than a way of remembering, it is a way of *being.* "This is the way we used to do things. Different from young people today," Gram will observe—not as a criticism of modern times, but as a way to define who she is and to tell others where she has come from.

> *Respect elders' stories and let them talk:*
> *The telling is integral to their identities.*

USE IT OR LOSE IT

I don't do cartwheels any more, but I still do a barre to keep supple.

Marie Rambert

The body needs exercise at any age. Movement and activity keep us healthy and engaged in life's events. According to the National Institutes of Health, exercise is "the most effective anti-aging pill ever discovered." Even people who've never exercised much in their lives can benefit from beginning exercise programs in their later years. It really *is* a matter of better late than never: Studies show that sedentary adults can boost their aerobic capacity twenty percent by beginning to exercise regularly—this means they'll be moving around with a vitality comparable to inactive people who are ten to twenty years younger.

It is important, though, for elders to choose exercise programs with the aid of a geriatrician or physical therapist who can tailor routines to individual fitness levels and states of health. Start slow and build from there. Encourage your loved one to tell health care professionals what kind of exercise he or she *likes* to do; some people would rather swim, while others prefer yoga, tennis, golf, low-impact aerobics, or weight lifting. Walking is good exercise, too. Exercise boosts your immune system, increases lung capacity, promotes cardiovascular fitness, builds muscle strength and endurance, and keeps you flexible, coordinated, and balanced. And, face it, moving around encourages participation in life, not just a witnessing of it.

Exercise brings youthful energy to a seasoned body.

DIET

Food is an important part of a balanced diet.

FRAN LEBOWITZ

A lot of elders, particularly if they live alone, don't eat properly. The body in age and illness requires a good, balanced diet to maintain the best state of health—plenty of fresh fruits, vegetables, and grains. Too many seniors rely on prepared foods, such as TV dinners and other frozen foods, which are generally high in fat, sugar, salt, and chemical preservatives. Some elders may still try to cook for themselves—my grandmother, Jessie, cooks when she can—but the effort can be exhausting. This is especially true for someone who suffers with chronic illness or is recovering from surgery. Elders have decreased manual dexterity and lack the strength for standing on their feet in front of the stove or the ability to lift and handle heavy pots and pans.

If you know your parent or grandparent should be eating better, there are several alternatives. Hire a neighbor to cook extra and deliver healthy meals to your loved one. If you live in an urban center, good take-out food is only a phone call away, and you can establish a relationship with one or two local restaurants. Many grocery stores deliver. And several good catalog mail-order services for organic food staples and produce exist now that can be wonderful resources for fresh, nutritious foods delivered regularly, right to your parent's doorstep.

Nutritrious foods are vital fuels that jump-start elders' bodies,
adding life to their years and years to their lives.

GETTING A LIFE

I tell you, hopeless grief is passionless.

ELIZABETH BARRETT BROWNING

My boyfriend Tom's father is a robust, enthusiastic man in his early seventies; Walt Kwiczola is enjoying his life. But Dad Kwiczola's rebirth in late life has come at a price: His wife, Ethel, died in 1987 from breast cancer. For almost a year, Walt went through the motions of living. But the evenings were hard and lonely without Ethel.

One Friday night, Walt said to himself, "What the hell am I doing, sitting around the house by myself?" He got up, shaved, put on a sport coat, and went to a local restaurant/bar he had gone to with his wife early in their marriage. Eating dinner at the bar, Walt noticed several other patrons who seemed just like him—older people returning to familiar haunts of the past, looking to find new doors to the future. They started to talk. Walt realized that honoring his life partner didn't have to mean accepting loneliness or isolation in late life.

Walt is now president of his local Widow and Widower's Club and has a companion, Edee; they travel together, go out to dinner together, and they love to go dancing. Dad Kwiczola drives a hard bargain—especially when negotiating for his club, playing it to the hilt with the salesclerk: "This CD player is for the widows and widowers; you want the seniors to have dances, don't you?" These days, Walt spends Friday nights leading the macarena at the senior center.

For every grieving person there is a community of peers
who are waiting to welcome and befriend.

LIVING WILLS

Death will come, always out of season.

Chief Big Elk

W hy do I need to make out one of those?" Mom insisted. "Of course the doctors are going to do everything to keep me alive and then I'll get well. And that's what you'll tell them to do anyway. What else is there *to* tell them?"

"I'm not going to give my body to science. No way," my grandmother, Jessie, said.

Explaining living wills and durable powers of attorney for health care to my mother and grandmother was no easy task. A living will is a legal document in which you can express your treatment wishes should you become incapacitated by an end-stage condition or terminal illness and not have the ability to express those wishes yourself. Physicians and hospitals are bound by law to honor your living will. A durable power of attorney for health care is a separate document that applies only to health and medical treatment issues, not finances and money. When you appoint a trusted person in this role you are giving him or her the legal right to make medical treatment decisions on your behalf; it can go into effect immediately, or only in the event that you can't make the decisions yourself. A durable power of attorney for health care is a wise document for your aging parent to execute.

My mother finally gave in. The specter of the dementia associated with her case of Parkinson's frightened her; ultimately, it made Mom feel safe to know that even if she became mentally incompetent her wishes would be honored through her living will. As for my eighty-eight-year-old grandmother, whenever I bring up the subject, her answer is: "I'm not afraid to die. I'll go when God wants me and not a minute sooner. No piece of paper can change God's will."

In our imperfect world, a living will is an intimate instruction of trust that preserves the dignity of our wishes.

POA

—

You see what power is—
holding someone else's fear in your hand
and showing it to them!

AMY TAN

Legal and financial powers of attorney are controversial issues in most families. POAs are legal documents authorizing a person or persons to make legal decisions on behalf of another person, as the agent acting for the grantor. A legal and financial power of attorney and a power of attorney for health care can be granted in the same document. My mother and I argued a long time about the need to appoint a POA to represent her interests. "I can make my own decisions," she said. "Besides, you and your brother's names are on all the bank accounts already; what else could you need?"

I explained to Mom that a power of attorney means more than just writing checks—powers of attorney give grantees the right to close and open bank accounts, disburse IRA funds, sign legal documents, and deal with insurance, government, and tax issues. Most importantly for anyone who might suffer the effects of progressive dementia, powers of attorney must be appointed while the grantor is mentally competent and must be in force for a number of years specified by law before the grant cannot be contested. This is done to protect the grantor's interests, the same way a person's last will and testament must be written while he or she is "in sound mind." The laws governing POAs may vary from jurisdiction to jurisdiction, so be sure to check with a lawyer about power of attorney agreements where you live.

Convinced of the advantages, Mom needed to decide who she wanted her POA to be. Choosing a POA representative is a personal and intimate decision. My mother granted her POA to me, her daughter. It is a choice that has not set easily with my brother, Mike. Already estranged from each other, Mom and Mike grew further apart. And Mom's decision fostered Mike's impression that I had control of Mom's life. It has taken Mike and me years to work through it all and to strengthen our own relationship.

There is a lot of fear of exploitation associated with the granting of powers of attorney. Perhaps this is because we live in a society where a power granted is perceived as an asset lost, imperiled, and not as a responsibility, a trust of care we bestow. I will tell you this: If Mom had not acted to appoint a power of attorney when she did, her affairs would have become truly a nightmare inheritance for her children. If your parent becomes mentally incompetent without a legal power of attorney in place in full force, you must go to court to petition for your parent's legal guardianship in order to have the right to take care of his or her affairs.

POAs are meant to preserve and sustain
an elder's rights and dignity,
not to exploit or impoverish them.

NOT ME

There is no such thing as a natural death . . .
for every man his death is an accident and, even if he knows it
and consents to it, an unjustifiable violation.

<small>SIMONE DE BEAUVOIR</small>

My cousin T.J. has one of the gentlest faces and manners I have ever known. I remember thinking this when the priest arrived to say last rites in the hospital for my mother's mother. T.J. and I stood on either side of Gram Granger. We held her hands, our heads bent together over her bed, our bodies constructing a doorframe between this world and the next. It was just our luck to be the ones in the room at that moment.

"Sylvia, I'm here to say the last rites," the priest told my grandmother. As he anointed her, my grandmother turned her head away. T.J. and I prayed out loud with the priest and I thought, *So this is what it is like.* "No," my grandmother said. "No."

Sylvia Granger did not believe she was dying. A mental feat of some magnitude, given the state her body was in. Anyone could see it. Why couldn't she? For some people, death is unimaginable, untenable. Sylvia's death was almost more exhausting, I think, for us—the ones who had to watch her violent struggle—than for her. Her children, my mother and uncle, I know, lost something of themselves in the effort, too.

T.J. and I never speak about those last rites, that gateway we held strong and gentle for Sylvia, who did not want to pass through.

Life has one undeniable fact: Every living thing must die.

FOR THE LONG TERM

The word "now" is like a bomb through the window, and it ticks.

ARTHUR MILLER

When we think about the future, we certainly do not picture ourselves or our aging parents in nursing homes. My mother, even knowing that Parkinson's disease would most likely someday incapacitate her, never believed she would need nursing home care. *It's not going to happen to me.*

True, none of us can predict the future. But if someone you love must live with a chronic illness such as painful osteoarthritis, the damaging physical or mental aftermath of stroke, or the progressive dementia of Alzheimer's, it is safe to assume that a greater level of care will someday be required. Maybe right now you and your parent have the resources you need to take care of things. But it is prudent to look down the road.

In my experience, as a parent declines, opportunities narrow. Money gets tighter, taking decisions about care and treatment options increasingly out of your hands. Legal issues become more problematic—if your loved one becomes mentally incompetent to manage finances and has established no power of attorney, it will be tremendously difficult to take care of business. Health issues escalate; managing care can become overwhelming if your parent requires constant attention and can no longer perform the activities of daily living. Start researching retirement communities, health insurance options, hospice and home care, financial and legal issues today. A little farther down the road, you'll be glad you did.

Compel the future, before it compels you.

MONEY

*Money is like a sixth sense without which you cannot
make a complete use of the other five.*

SOMERSET MAUGHAM

Sometimes, it seems our greatest hurdle in the care of our aging parents is money. Everything costs money. If our parents need care and there is no money to provide it, lack of money shapes our decisions. If our parents do have some money, our decisions can't help but consider where the money goes and why. Nursing homes typically cost thirty thousand dollars or more per year of care. A professional round-the-clock live-in caregiver costs just as much. We watch as our parents' life savings are wiped out in a year or two to meet Medicaid's spend-down requirements, or face the stress and overwhelming responsibility of providing their care ourselves, with only minimal assistance from outside sources. Where in this reality is the American dream our parents worked a lifetime to achieve for themselves, the American dream they worked so hard to pass on to their children?

As the baby-boom generation swells the ranks of older Americans, long-term care reform will force its way through Congress. Surely, a system that allows its citizens to lose in a heartbeat everything they have endeavored over a lifetime to accomplish *must* be reformed.

*Write to your congressional representatives and
tell them about your family's struggle to provide good care.
Advocate for long-term care reform!*

RETIREMENT

—

My voice had a long, nonstop career.
It deserves to be put to bed with quiet and dignity,
not yanked out every once in a while to see
if it can still do what it used to do. It can't.

BEVERLY SILLS

As our parents, and their parents before them, worked hard through their middle years, retirement beckoned as a long-awaited sigh of relaxation. A time to sit. A time to play. A time to let the next generation do all the huffing and puffing and running around. Indeed, for our parents and grandparents, the accomplishment of having stayed alive long enough to reach retirement may seem justification enough for kicking back and taking it slow. Remember, at the beginning of the twentieth century, the average lifespan was forty-five years. Times have changed!

Today, some elders use retirement as a time to take off and just keep going, while others may feel the pressure is on to be lively and entertaining when all they want to do is sit down and enjoy the show. Whichever category our aging parents choose, as long as they are happy and productive, and take good care of their health, encourage them to do what they want.

Retirement means earning the freedom
to enjoy life at your own pace.

ACHES AND PAINS

Time and trouble will tame an advanced young woman,
but an advanced old woman is uncontrollable by any earthly force.

DOROTHY SAYERS

My father's mother is an incredible, indomitable woman. In the course of my thirty-eight years of life, I have never witnessed any one person with more talent than Jessie at stirring things up. It is exhaustingly true, even today. At eighty-eight, Jessie is a housebound tornado waiting to touch down on anyone who rings her doorbell, particularly if that someone is one of her grandchildren, Mike or me, visiting from California or New York.

"I hate it that I can't walk like I used to," Jessie complains. "I have such aches and pains. I want to go, go, go. I need a vacuum cleaner and a pair of black shoes, and, oh, so many things."

"Well, why don't you get a wheelchair in the house? Medicare will pay for it. That way we can throw it in the car and go anywhere, anytime, without depending on walking or whether a wheelchair is available where we're going. We'll get one of those disabled parking passes to put in the windshield of the car. Anyone who takes you out can use it to make parking easier. You'll be able to leave the house without it being such a big production." Silence from Jessie, who is rubbing holy water on her arthritic knee. Jessie believes the body is a house of prayer. "Or I could go out and buy some things for you and bring them here—we could even order from catalogs."

"I want to be able to see what I'm getting and pick it out myself. And those catalogs are no good. Besides, I don't want to bother anybody. I want to do things for myself."

Ooookayyyy . . . Suddenly, I feel such sympathy for my father, growing up with this.

"I'm fifty years older than you, granddaughter. I have my way of doing things and you children have yours, you see. And that's it!" She grabs my face in her hands, "But we love each other, don't we?" More than you know, Gram; best friends.

The time you spend together may accomplish
more than you think.

TOUCH ME. FEEL ME.

Love consists in this, that two solitudes protect
and touch and greet each other.

RAINER MARIA RILKE

I love to watch the movie *The Producers*, especially the part at the beginning where Zero Mostel shamelessly bilks old ladies out of their money, seducing them by playing outrageous love games. "Touch me. Feel me," one old lady croons to Zero, who rolls his eyes back in his head and proceeds to lay claim to her checkbook.

Physical touch is a profound method of human connection and communication (one that Zero took humorous but improper advantage of!). From shaking hands to hugging to a kiss on the cheek, touch engages our senses in awareness and gives us an intimate platform for expressing our feelings. When touch is performed merely as duty or a superficial routine, the message communicated is one of disinterest or indifference. No one likes mechanical affection. Everyone craves the feeling of belonging that the human bond of touch can provide. Scientific studies confirm that physical touch and psychological well-being are inextricably intertwined in the human experience. Even if you are uncomfortable with or unused to outward displays of affection, your efforts to touch can communicate that you care about the people who are important to you, and may help you open up to your own feelings. Let the power of touch deepen and enrich your relationship with your aging parent or grandparent who may be longing for a hug today.

Touch is our umbilical cord to life, to each other.

LONELINESS

The most I ever did for you was to outlive you. But that is much.

EDNA ST. VINCENT MILLAY

I have a friend I have known since I was five years old, over thirty years now. No one knows me better, or at least knows more about me. . . . Our fathers died within a few years of each other, and, for the next decade, our mothers defined themselves as "widow." Diane's mother is gone now, too. When Marge was sick, Mom and I accompanied Diane on a hospital visit. Our mothers talked about their lives. "Gloria, I guess I never got over Gus's death," Marge said. "I could never get past it. And I never wanted to. I know I'm not supposed to say that, but it's how I feel." I saw Mom's eyes filling up with tears as she turned her wedding band around and around in circles on her finger. "I miss Joe," she said. The weight of the grief and the loneliness in that room seemed unbearable.

"What does it mean to be whole?" I asked Diane later that night over coffee at the Double-T diner, an old familiar haunt. "Our lives are connected to the people we share them with. So, who understands who we are when those people are gone?"

"But, Lee," Diane answered, "is wholeness really about other people understanding us, or is it how we feel about ourselves?" We talked for hours about grief, love, change, moving on. Life.

Loneliness is the poverty of self.
Reach out.

MOVING CLOSER

Call it a clan, call it a network, call it a tribe, call it a family.
Whatever you call it, whoever you are, you need one.

JANE HOWARD

My family struggles with the demands and rigors of long-distance caregiving. Mom and Gram are in Baltimore. But Mike lives in California now and I live in New York. The expectation that I'd eventually move "home" to Baltimore has followed me throughout the caregiving experience. Our society still pressures women to this role, and my own family has sent mixed signals—encouraging me to live my own life and at the same time calling me back. But even Mike feels the pull, speaking to Gram every day on the phone to help her feel connected to her family.

My uncle Donald and aunt Mary, Mom's brother and his wife, live close by and visit regularly, helping with day-to-day care. Long-distance caregivers can also take advantage of local resources, such as geriatric care managers who help locate and provide specific services your aging parent or grandparent may need. Your local Area Agency on Aging can also give good advice on where to turn for help within your community.

Before deciding to move your parent closer to you or to move yourself closer to your parent, give long-distance caregiving a fair try while you think through all the ramifications of uprooting your family. Then, if you decide that moving is right for you, proceed with a clear mind, heart, and focus.

Networks of care sustain families across the miles.

SELF-HELP

No one wants advice—only corroboration.

JOHN STEINBECK

I have a shelf full of books related to children of aging parents written by all types of experts: health care journalists, social workers, physicians, organizations and advocates devoted to aging issues, professional caregivers. The books have great information and I've used something at least once from all of them. Yet I often find this shelf of books daunting and depressing. How could I possibly do *all* of the things these books recommend? Am I a bad child if I don't? And what if the advice isn't *practical?* One book suggested calling an older person at medication times and holding on the phone until you are sure the dose is taken. Sounds like a good idea. But how many of us, whether we work in an office or take care of our families at home, have time to do this every four hours, every day, every month, every year? I eye that shelf of books and I know I'll never have enough time or energy to put every recommendation into action. Let's face it, we're not that organized and creative in dealing with our *own* lives. The best we can do is to take the ideas we need from the resources we find and use them to help our parents, while at the same time preserving a measure of normalcy in our own lives.

Use resources to confirm your path and to help make the way a little smoother, not rougher.

ROLLER COASTER

I remember the sheer terror and excitement I felt as a child going on a roller coaster ride. The rush of adrenaline, pounding heart, slow climb, fear of heights, and exhilaration of speed. The shocks and thrills of an unpredictable ride that ends without warning, as quickly as it began.

Mom's Parkinson's has got to be the wildest ride I've ever been on. With each challenge Mom and I faced we looked forward with hope, dread, determination—a whole host of feelings. When we sold Mom's house and moved her to the retirement community I worked so hard to make sure everything was set up just right for her, envisioning several happy years of good living before the Parkinson's made the next level of care necessary. I thought the ride was over for a while, but only six months later Mom's Parkinson's had her life out of control again—she couldn't medicate herself, she had frequent falls, and her judgment grew poorer and poorer. We realized that we had to consider giving up Mom's independent living apartment and moving to the retirement community's assisted living facility. Welcome to another wild ride on the Parkinson's Express.

I came to find out that Mom's life would never be stable again, that no matter how much effort I put in, she would continue to decline and what had been done would be undone and done and undone again and again with each new development. For a while, this took the heart out of living for me:

I became filled with despair and fear—nothing good or hopeful seemed possible from this roller coaster experience, only horror and stress with grief and loss as the ultimate payoff.

I had missed the point from the beginning: This ride was never about "fixing" Mom's life, of supporting the unsupportable truth of Mom's Parkinson's—but about loving her and accompanying her through the ups and downs, holding her hand during the scary moments, laughing during the exhilarating moments of success, making the best of it, and resting together on the sidelines as we wait for the next roller coaster car to come along and take us for another unpredictable ride. Hang on!

Love keeps us on track through the long-anticipated free falls,
the peaceful lulls, and the harrowing hairpin turns life brings.

FOR BETTER OR WORSE

All tragedies are finished by a death,
All comedies are ended by a marriage;
The future states of both are left to faith.

GEORGE GORDON, THE SIXTH LORD BYRON

Caring for an aging parent or grandparent can put tremendous strain on a relationship or marriage. Even if your parent does not live with you, the constant phone calls, errands, visits, and accompanying stress drags your attention away from your family's daily routines. You are torn between your partner and your parent, who both—in the best and worst of circumstances—compete every day for your loyalty, love, and time. If you have children, feel free to multiply the demands exponentially. It is tremendously difficult to support the realities of so many different worlds; nobody does it well for long.

I've never been married, and at thirty-eight I know that part of the reason has to do with the care I've offered my parents: my father's cancer in my twenties and Mom's Parkinson's in my thirties. I chose relationships with men who were emotionally distant, not interested in commitment, unavailable when it came time to help. And if they did want to help, I pushed them away. Somehow, I thought if I kept my worlds separate, I could insulate my heart against the shocks of loss. But of course it doesn't work that way; whatever happens in one place spills over. So I am learning how to integrate my worlds, to welcome and trust the ineffable goodness of the people in my life.

Instead of splitting yourself apart,
allow the people you love to help keep you whole.

89

SUPPORT

That sense of being in the same boat is really a very powerful thing when you're dealing with something that's difficult.

DR. DAVID SPIEGEL, STANFORD UNIVERSITY SCHOOL OF MEDICINE

Caring for an aging parent or grandparent, we can feel isolated and overwhelmed. We don't have many socially acceptable outlets we can depend on to talk about our feelings or to discuss the things that happen to us or to our parents. It may seem easier to go undercover, put our emotions on autopilot, and say to ourselves, *Let's just get through it.*

No problem, this secret life of struggle and loss. We may even feel that telling the truth about what it is like to care for our parents is somehow an invasion of their privacy, a betrayal of their dignity and former vitality. And joining a support group or talking to a therapist, well, that's for people who are emotionally weak, who are unable to handle *anything* themselves.

I tell you what, the most amazing discovery I made in a support group is this: No matter how different people are, their experiences are universal. Real emotional strength, real power, comes from human connections, from sharing what happens to us. It's the same kind of instantaneous relief we feel when we travel to a foreign country and suddenly, for the first time on our journey, we encounter a group of fellow travelers who speak our language, who understand us and with whom we can exchange experiences and advice.

Common experiences bring people together.
Add your voice to the group.

HOME IMPROVEMENTS

Housekeeping ain't no joke.

LOUISA MAY ALCOTT

Every now and then my grandmother will horrify me with some story about wanting to get up on a ladder and clean the chandeliers. I think she just likes trying to shock me, though I know she'd get up there herself and bring that crystal down to wash it if she thought she could get away with it. "I'm just having a conversation with you," Jessie will say. "I know what's safe to do."

But seniors' ideas of their own physical limitations and *our* ideas or their *physicians'* ideas may be worlds apart. People who've prided themselves on their homes will have trouble letting go of heavy-duty housekeeping activities—finding the mental distress of an imperfect home more upsetting than the potential dangers of physical exertion. Gram gets exhausted just vacuuming the living room floor. Injuries from falls or over-exertion, such as broken bones, respiratory distress, or heart attack, are all serious, life-threatening events for the elderly.

As our parents and grandparents age, we need to help them recognize potential hazards in their environment and encourage them to get a housekeeper to do all but the lightest of tasks. One of the best ways to do this is to have a licensed physical therapist visit your parent's home. The therapist can give you great suggestions for "elder-proofing," while preserving as many of your loved one's routines and physical surroundings as possible.

A safe home is a haven that nurtures and protects our elders.

ALL FUNCTIONS GO

The mind and the heart sometimes get another chance, but if anything happens to the poor old human frame, why, it's just out of luck, that's all.

KATHERINE ANNE PORTER

The retirement community my mom lives in offers three levels of care: independent living, the apartments; assisted living, the dormitory; and the care center, the nursing home. The distinction between residents in each level of the community is more or less determined by the state of the body and mind. Independent living units at life care communities are like apartment complexes. Elders here are active, relatively healthy people who can lead autonomous lives with minimal or occasional support.

When physical or mental decline makes it harder for an elder to lead a normal life without daily support, assisted living is the choice of care. In a dormitory setting, residents still retain a sense of independence and community but are close to the supervising care needed for people who have trouble walking or self-medicating, or are too confused to get around safely by themselves. Residents may stay in assisted living arrangements until they require constant skilled nursing care or are no longer able to "toilet" themselves. This doesn't mean incontinence that is controlled by an elder who wears pads or makes frequent, unsupervised trips to a bathroom; it means losing the mental or physical ability to use the bathroom at all. This second type of incontinence is not allowed in assisted living arrangements and will necessitate nursing home care.

It can be hard to accept that facilities will admit your parent based on what seems such a gross assessment of physical and mental capability. It was my mom's inability to toilet herself that prevented her from enjoying the benefits of the assisted living level of care at the community. Mom moved directly from her apartment to the care center.

But we tried. Home health aides worked with Mom to help her confused mind "relearn" toileting skills. We even posted step-by-step instructions by the toilet for her to follow. She said to me once as we followed the list, "When did they change the way to do this? It was so much easier before." We struggled until we had to accept the inevitable. Still, I firmly believe in the promise of retirement communities: These communities offer elders the chance to get the most out of life by providing support tailored to meet their individual health needs.

*When the body is cared for appropriately, the mind
and the heart are encouraged to flourish.*

THE TUNE WITHOUT WORDS

"Hope" is the thing with feathers—
That perches in the soul—
And sings the tune without the words—
And never stops—at all—

EMILY DICKINSON, #254

Sometimes, it is hard to know what to hope for. Some people even say it can be dangerous to hope, foolish to dream. But hope is a kind of renewal, a voice within us that speaks directly to our hearts about our deepest desires and wishes with a conviction that has no use for words; it is an abiding certainty, continuing.

When we suspect that our hope may be further than our grasp, when we watch someone we love move down a path of illness, of mental or physical deterioration, a feeling of despair can creep into our hearts. At this time, when we are in danger of becoming lost, we need to stand still, to listen more closely for the voice of hope carried within us. For hope is abiding. Hope, the smallest creature, can speak to us through a glance of recognition, the smile of a shared memory, the peace and acceptance of loving while we can, however we are able. We will discover that our hope is as powerful and moving as ever before. And we will find the strength to soar once more.

Hope is a song of love, taking flight in our souls.

HONORING THE DIFFICULT

The truth does not change according to our ability to stomach it emotionally.

FLANNERY O'CONNOR

Some people walk around constructing elaborate pathways to detour a fact of life that just doesn't fit in with their ideas about themselves, their relationships, and how they think their lives should be. And when an unmistakable truth creates an impasse, some people pretend to be blind and hope eventually it will simply fade away. Hunkered down and sticking to their own stories, some people wait for unpleasant truths to pass out of their lives and rejoice when difficult times are "over" and can be "forgotten." But what price do we pay when we lack the emotional strength to welcome not only the good times in our lives, but the hard times as well?

I could never understand this impulse to erase whole sections of experience, as if difficult times have nothing to teach us, no honor or reward. Difficult life experiences can enrich our lives if we take the effort to let them transform us, if we act to learn from the difficult and grow by embracing our experiences honestly. Maybe I feel this way because my mother is one of those people who cannot honor the difficult. "Do you think people would know I have Parkinson's?" Mom says, looking me in the eye from her wheelchair in the nursing home, twenty years after her diagnosis. "Yes, Mom," I tell her. "I think they would." And then she looks away from me, her impasse.

If we deny what is difficult in our lives, we devalue our own life experiences; we ignore the rich textures of our unique life fabrics.

MOMENT OF TRUTH

All my possessions for a moment of time.

ELIZABETH I

"My life is more important than yours," Mom says to me. She does not want to stay in the nursing home. She rips her wrist bracelet off her arm and blames me. "You have to help me get out of here. I won't stay here." Her wide blue eyes lock into mine. We had reached the inexorable moment when our elaborate efforts to prop up and support Mom's life were no longer good enough. It had all collapsed in a ruin.

"I can't make it right anymore, Mom. Everything's not all right. And it's not going to be." And then I did something I had never done before. I just turned around and walked out. I drove to the house I grew up in on Kirkwood Road and sat parked across the street for a long time. I went to seek advice from Mom's best friend, Miss Jean; from my childhood friend Diane; and then from my grandmother, Jessie. Hours later, I returned to my mother in the nursing home.

"I'm sorry, Mom," I said. I cried and my mother held me in her arms.

"I know," she said. "I know." That day we began to build in a new direction.

Parent and child, we sustain each other through life,
building for the duration.

DEPRESSION

*Depression has its own angel, a guiding spirit whose job
it is to carry the soul away to remote places
where it finds unique insight and enjoys special vision.*

THOMAS MOORE

Depression is an uneasy, uncomfortable emotion. Usually, it is a state of mind we take great pains to get out of. Our friends, families, and coworkers don't want to hear that we're depressed or unhappy. These feelings are "unacceptable." And if we can't lift our depression, we try to suppress it, spiraling our sadness inward until we feel hopelessly isolated and alone.

Caring for an aging parent is grueling, relentless work: a hundred miles of hard road, as a friend of mine once put it. We need to realize that we are not caught in a lonely downward spiral as we walk this road with our aging parents. Every parent and child who makes this journey shares the same feelings of loss, depression, and grief. Anyone who doesn't feel this way isn't human. Accept your feelings of sadness and allow yourself to deeply experience each nuance of emotion. You may find that what you learn about yourself and your parent as you explore your troubled emotions and embrace your difficult circumstances has a strangely healing power.

*Understanding sadness can move us to great compassion and wisdom:
a rebirth of the heart and soul forged by pain and love.*

IN THE ELEVATOR

*We do not grow absolutely, chronologically. . . . The past, present,
and future mingle and pull us backward, forward, or fix us in the present.
We are made up of layers, cells, constellations.*

ANAÏS NIN

I am holding a pot of white daisies for Mom. I know she has been waiting for me all day. I am not alone. Another woman rides with me; she carries red geraniums. She looks to be about my mother's age: sixty-four. As people do in elevators, we begin to exchange pleasantries. She is visiting her mother.

"What do you do?" she asks me. "Are you one of the social workers?"

"No," I say. "I am here to see my mother, too." We look into each other's eyes, filled, suddenly, with tears. Neither of us can say, *So young.* The woman squeezes my fingers with a mother's touch. I feel myself sinking, but the elevator moves, taking us up. I try to smile at the woman; I hold her hand, encourage her. The elevator doors open and we move apart,— one going south, the other north, for our visits. We know we will meet each other again.

That evening, as I walk to my car, I glance up to the fourth floor of the care center and see in the dim window light from two of the rooms, daisies and geraniums lifting their heads to the moon and the stars on a warm summer night in June.

*Compassion does not know the boundaries of time, age, or relationship.
It grows through the conduit of love.*

LOOK IN YOUR HAND

Do not leave my hand without light.

MARC CHAGALL

We all remember as children dipping our hands into brightly colored paints, pressing our palms to white paper. The prints we left there identified us—red, blue, yellow, green. Today, we watch as our children bring their handprints home from school, discovering, too, who they are.

As adults, we concern ourselves with using our hands. We know who we are: We are the ones who lift, carry, shape, build, pull, push, feed, instruct, protect, console, create. Our hands are made to work, are made to make things happen.

As we grow older, our hands may begin to ache with a lifetime of use. Simple tasks become more difficult. So we learn to reach our hands toward one another with a new purpose. Holding the hands of our daughters and sons in our warm grasp, the strength of our hands' experience steadies our children and gives them hope.

My grandmother, mother, and I sit in the activity room at the nursing home. Carefully Jessie lifts Mom's hand while I spread her fingers. Mom's palm dips into the blue paint and settles on white paper. Gram laughs and presses a red palm to the paper. My own hand is green. We look into those hands, the prints of three generations of women. I know myself. And I am never alone.

In your hand lies the strength of generations.

RIGHT OF REFUSAL

Never give in, never give in, never, never, never, never—
in nothing, great or small, large or petty—never give in
except to convictions of honor and good sense.

WINSTON CHURCHILL

Treatment decisions can be hard when your aging parent or grandparent won't cooperate. Legally, every individual has the right to refuse treatment. Just because you think your loved one should get a certain drug, therapy, or surgery doesn't mean that health care professionals, even if they agree with you, will listen to you and administer the care over the objections of your parent, as long as your parent is mentally competent to make his or her own decisions.

That said, a physician will strongly advocate for needed care. If your aging parent or grandparent is refusing care that both you *and* the physician feel is warranted and necessary, contact the doctor directly to work out a plan of persuasion. Get a second medical opinion to add to the consensus for care. Sometimes it is hard to even *get* an older person *into* a doctor's office, much less get them to pursue a recommended course of treatment.

Remember that your loved one is being asked to make intimate decisions about the integrity of his or her body that deserve consideration and respect. Be patient and keep talking it through. Given time, you'll both recognize the right thing to do.

We all hold the individual right and responsibility
to honor our bodies as we see fit.

INSURANCE

We have to act now to make sure you don't have to be a Rockefeller
to afford decent health care in this country.

JAY ROCKEFELLER

Today, the "rising cost of health care" we hear about so much in the news means that health care consumers— i.e., you and me—have less choice in our own care and pay higher premiums, deductibles, and out-of-pocket expenses in the bargain. While politicians, physicians, consumer advocates, and insurance companies fight it out in Washington, over-sixty-fivers cling to their "government mandate for health care": Medicare.

Seniors, however, should not rely on Medicare benefits alone to pay the costs of doctor's bills and hospital stays. If your parent is approaching sixty-five and is still employed, or covered in retirement by an employer's health insurance plan, research how and whether the plan remains in effect once Medicare kicks in. Supplemental insurance, or "Medigap" policies, covers what Medicare won't—including prescriptions and some out-of-pocket expenses. If your parent applies for Medigap insurance within six months of enrolling in Medicare Part B, he or she cannot be denied coverage because of pre-existing conditions.

Remember that Medicare and Medicaid are different. Medicare only rarely pays any benefits for long-term care in nursing homes; has "skilled" requirements, not monetary ones; and generally covers doctor and hospital bills. To qualify for government benefits through Medicaid for nursing home care, your parent must deplete personal assets—must "spend down"—to meet Medicaid's ever-evolving requirements. If your parent has a large estate, you can investigate the advantages of a long-term care insurance policy, to protect against the loss of assets in spend-down. These policies, however, are expensive—and your parent may be ineligible if he or she is already "too old" or has been diagnosed with a debilitating illness, such as Alzheimer's. Sometimes, elders can also cash in life insurance benefits to pay for nursing home care. A new phenomena are companies that pay fifty to eighty percent as a cash payout in order to be named as a policy's beneficiary. Congress now allows payouts up to $64,000 before taxing them (at least, as of this writing . . .).

If you suspect that long-term care may eventually be needed, talk to your parent about contacting a lawyer and financial planner as soon as possible to discuss the best way to handle assets and protect your parent's best interests. The more realistically you take a look at what *could* happen, the more influence you will have over what *does* happen. In the meantime, add your voice, and your parent's, to the national debate over medical insurance and long-term health care. After all, at the end of the day, these are *our* tax dollars at work and *our* health that's at stake.

> *Because the future holds no guarantees, we look to*
> *the protection and security insurance promises.*

THE OLD GENERAL

I must govern the clock, not be governed by it.

GOLDA MEIR

"Excuse me. What time is it?"

"Just about five o'clock."

"Good. I have to ask because I don't have a watch anymore. Do you know what time dinner is around here?"

"Around five o'clock—so, any time now you should be going into the dining room."

"Great. Do you know what time it is?"

"Just about five o'clock."

"Good, because I just heard that dinner starts around five and I'm hungry."

I had this conversation with a lovely man on the same floor with my mother at the nursing home. I've affectionately dubbed him "the Old General" because he is a very tall, gray, imposing figure with a bellowing voice, curious nature, and a big heart. Like many other older people, the Old General is losing track of time. Not knowing what time it is, or even what day or month, can be extremely disorienting. Always try to respond with patience to elders' questions about time. Help elders by making a flip-card calendar with the day, month, and date in large printed letters: Saturday, February 15. Or decorate their rooms or homes with the trappings of the appropriate season; visual reminders are often more effective than numbers and words, written or spoken.

To every thing, there is a season,
and a time to every purpose under heaven.

DANCING WITH MR. MOONEY

Think of the magic of that foot, comparatively small,
upon which your whole weight rests. It's a miracle,
and the dance . . . is a celebration of that miracle.

MARTHA GRAHAM

Mr. Mooney has a room on the same floor as my mother at the nursing home. He is a tall, thin man in his early seventies, who, like my Mom, has Parkinson's disease. I wouldn't say that Mr. Mooney and Mom have struck up a friendship. When they meet, usually a chance encounter, they inspect each other with wide eyes—as if they've never seen someone else with Parkinson's before. Maybe they haven't.

The Parkinson's has both Mr. Mooney and Mom in a wheelchair most of the time now. But when I hold her hand, Mom walks like a ballerina: small, careful steps that rise onto her toes. She looks around like a small child who's about to be caught getting into something, that same expression of the new and undiscovered.

One Saturday night not so long ago, as I stepped off the elevator onto Mom's floor, there were Mom and Mr. Mooney, sitting in their wheelchairs in the open lounge. I don't know exactly how they came to be there. "What are you two planning?" I ask them. Mr. Mooney and Mom look each other over conspiratorily. Mom says, "A party."

"Dance with us, sweetie," Mr. Mooney invites me. Mom's slippered feet rise up onto her toes.

The heart will always remember how to dance.

GENEROSITY

Allah, Most High, says: he who approaches near to me one span,
I will approach to him one cubit; and he who approaches near to me one
cubit, I will approach near to him one fathom; and whoever approaches me
walking, I will come to him running, and he who greets me with sins
equivalent to the whole world, I will greet him with forgiveness equal to it.

MISHKAT-UL-MASABIH

I always thought I knew what it meant to be generous, how it is better to give than to receive and all of that stuff about being nice to people. And I've always thought of myself as a generous, kind person. I put money in the poor box at church and I carry oranges in my bag to give to homeless people on the subway. But I never *really* understood about generosity until I found myself in need.

I cannot express how grateful I am to the people in my life who have offered kindness and assistance to me and to my mother in times of need—people who gave of their time and resources not just because they loved me or my family but simply because *we needed help.* It is humbling to reach out to others to accept the help we need. It is also the most empowering moment of all: to see hands reaching out to clasp ours, to sustain and buoy us through hard times. Because I know what it means to receive, I have learned at last what it means to give. To give without prejudice, reluctance, or conditions. To give, simply because someone needs help.

There is truly no distinction between giver and receiver,
only a shared humanity.

THE AWAKENING MIND

*Whether your experience at the time of death is positive or negative
is very much dependent on how you have practiced during your life.
The important thing is that our day-to-day life should be meaningful,
that our attitude should be positive, happy, and warm.*

HIS HOLINESS THE DALAI LAMA OF TIBET

We face death with dread and loathing. Many people die alone in hospitals, cared for by strangers—a prospect we all find horrifying, yet often feel powerless to influence. We long to control the process of our dying, but the idea of preparing mentally to embrace the experience of death as an important, inevitable life passage is rejected, fearful even to consider. Dying well is often viewed as a death free of pain and burden to others, and not as a death fully experienced by ourselves and our families as a part of what it means to be human, in essence, to be alive.

If we are awakened to the preciousness of life—living our lives fully and with care for others—our fears about dying may diminish. If every day we make it our duty to live well, actively cherishing and appreciating each moment and respecting the intrinsic value of the life of every other living being, perhaps we can cultivate the courage to face death with the same openness, cherishing and sharing each moment of life together until the very last. Our connections to each other become that much more vital, and we can offer each other support and encouragement as we all move through the time of our lives.

Tomorrow, or the next life, you never know which will come first.

ARTIFACTS

—

WILLIAM STAFFORD, "ALLEGIANCES"

There aren't words powerful enough to describe the emotion we invest in the objects of our lives. When we open the pages of a book or put a video into the VCR, the first scenes become an invitation into a world where each detail has some special, inherent meaning. We delight in discovering the meaning of the rose crystal vase on the mantelpiece or the swinging glider on the front porch. These details shape and define the characters,—and sometimes their destinies as well. In life, it is the same for us, though perhaps not as easily seen.

My house has become a hodgepodge collection of my things, my parents', my grandparents'. I live every day with their aura. Somewhere, under my skin, the knowledge of them lingers— sometimes uneasily, sometimes to comfort and console.

Every so often, I carry some special object to my mother when I visit. This time it is an inlaid music box we bought on a trip to Italy shortly after my father died. Our only vacation together, mother and daughter. She holds the music box in her hands and her eyes light with recognition. Her fingers are not steady enough to turn the key. "Play the music for me," she says.

Draw strength from the things that belong to your family.
Cherish them for the information they hold—
about your loved ones and about yourself.

POSITIVE ATTITUDE

No one is so old as to think he cannot live one more year.

Marcus Tullius Cicero

My grandmother wants to live to be one hundred. She's got twelve more years to go. On some days I marvel over her independence and determined spirit at age eighty-eight. On other days I wonder what quality of life can satisfy a woman whose old body must be bargained with at every step. "What is your secret?" I ask her. I am thinking: *How did you ever live to be so old?*

"Positive attitude!" Jessie blurts. Her face and voice are incredulous. *How could I not know this?* "Old people," she says, "have made it this far because they understand joy. You have *got* to think positive and believe that good things will happen to you." This from a woman who has outlived most all of her family. Gram has lost all of her brothers and sisters; her husband, a firefighter, in the line of duty; and her only child, my father, to cancer in the prime of his life. "Life isn't easy, granddaughter," she offers, "but it is *life*."

In the effort to take care of our elders, we have to remember their secret of healthy aging. Hold onto that positive attitude and bring on the years!

*Never give up on living. Hold onto the belief
that good things are yet to come.*

HOLIDAYS

Even if we spend a lot of money on gifts for everyone in our family, nothing we buy could give them as much happiness as the gift of our awareness, our smile. And this precious gift costs nothing.

THICH NHAT HANH

My family celebrates Christmas, and every year when I was growing up my mother would look upon it with dread. "How will I ever get everything ready on time? What if everyone doesn't like their presents? I don't think I have the energy to make all those cookies this year. . . ." And so forth and so on. Mom worried about everything, to the point where the celebration didn't seem enjoyable to her. Mom loved Christmas in her own way, but I wonder how our holidays would have been different if Mom had worried less and reveled more, if she could have slowed down enough to see in every small act, in every moment of life, cause for celebration, joy, and love.

Now, in her confusion, Mom has no sense of the passing of time. She may ask on any ordinary day, "Is it time for Thanksgiving?" The truth is, every moment can be a holiday, a gift shared with the people we love the most. And of course—we all know it, don't we?—the gift of our love is the most precious gift of all.

"We'll remind you," I tell her. "Good," she replies.

It is the gift we give from within ourselves, not without, that lasts a lifetime.

GETTING TO YES

To work in the world lovingly means that we are defining what we will be for, rather than reacting to what we are against.

CHRISTINA BALDWIN

Have you ever noticed how often we phrase our thoughts in negative terms? In one day, make a mental note of how many times you say the words *can't, won't, don't, shouldn't, couldn't.* In stressful or difficult situations, negative expressions can creep into our language and color our moods and our actions without our being fully aware of it. Everything is a problem. And it goes beyond us: If we are interacting with people who express themselves negatively, then we, too, can be drawn into a downward spiral of negative influences.

Listen to yourself. If what you are hearing is "no, No, NO," you need to start thinking more positively. Pay attention to the words you use; concentrate on choosing words that are active, engaging, and supportive. Look at the difference in these statements: "Dad, don't lift that heavy box yourself. Stop it. Give it to me; you'll only hurt your back and I can't spend the whole day fetching and carrying for you." "Dad, I know you prefer doing things by yourself, but lifting heavy boxes will hurt your back. You want to enjoy all the things you planned to do today. It's okay to ask for help. Let me help you." *Listen* to others. If someone around you is forever complaining, rephrase their complaints back to them using positive language—you'll be surprised at how effective this subliminal mood adjuster can be!

Accentuate the positive.

PULLING EARTHWARD

The heavier the burden, the closer our lives come to the earth, the closer our lives come to the earth, the more real and truthful they become.

MILAN KUNDERA

Ten years ago, I sat at my father's bedside and watched him die of cancer. My mother, grandmother, and I cared for Dad at home in those last weeks. I was twenty-five, and I needed my father alive. I put out a lifeline, believing that as long as that line held we would be forever linked. We would slip by the mysteries of life and death together. Two days before he died I felt that line snap back into my hands. In those last two days, I watched, incredulous, as my earthward pull, too strong for my father's frail body, rooted me more firmly among the living while my father floated weightless, pushing off the senses. And he was gone.

Today, at a slower, more agonizing pace, I am losing my mother to Parkinson's disease. And only now do I recognize the truth of what I'd discovered at my father's deathbed. You cannot make another person live through force of will. And you cannot die with them. What survives is love. Mom and I face each other. I relax Mom's stiffened fingers and hold her frail hands in mine. We count out loud together and I slowly pull her up from her wheelchair to a standing position. She floats, pressing down on my fingertips. We balance, still in a circle of life.

Gravity: The force of attraction by which terrestrial bodies tend to fall toward the center of the earth.

MINDFULNESS

*When it comes right down to it, the challenge of mindfulness
is to realize that "this is it." Right now is my life.*

JON KABAT-ZINN, PH.D., STRESS REDUCTION CLINIC,
UNIVERSITY OF MASSACHUSETTS MEDICAL CENTER

My mind is a list of things to do, and I tick them off with an almost imperceptible nod of the head: Check the laundry hamper, remember to take Mom's winter coat home for storage, make sure she is signed up for a hair appointment, leave a message for the physical therapist, give her a quick manicure. I virtually forget where I am and what I am doing. Driving to the nursing home for a visit with Mom, my life is a blur.

Sound familiar? We are busy people with too much on our minds and too many things to do. Stress, oh, yes—but excuse me, it's too stressful to find time to relax! We spend our lives with very little physical or emotional connection to the present moment—except how to get through it. Yet "right now" is the only moment we have. Focus on what you are doing *right now.* Observe what you are thinking *right now,* how your body feels *right now.* Try to live one moment at a time, instead of hours, days, weeks ahead of where you are.

Peace is every step.

AGE SPOTS

When grace is joined by wrinkles, it is adorable.
There is an unspeakable dawn in happy old age.

VICTOR HUGO

"I have this rash all over my body and it itches something ter-
rible," my grandmother, Jessie, tells me over the phone.

"Did you ask the doctor about it?"

"No, but I will the next time I see him."

✳

"Did you ask the doctor about that rash?"

"He says it's nothing, but I don't believe him. It's *all over my*
body and it itches. He said I should talk to you about it." Talk
to *me* about it? Since when did I get a medical degree . . . ?

"Okay, we'll look at it together the next time I come down
to Baltimore."

✳

The minute I enter Jessie's house her arm is in my face.
"Look at this rash. All over my face, my arms, my legs. It's ter-
rible. And nobody will do anything about it!" Age spots: I
am looking at brown liver spots on her arm—spots that have
been there for years.

"Gram, those are age spots. You've had them for years."

"Like hell they are. And I never had these until last month.
Age spots are for *old* people."

"News flash: You are old. As for the age spots, well, until
you had your cataracts out you just couldn't *see* them. But

they've been there for a long time. And I think they add character. You look beautiful."

Jessie looks at me and I know she is thinking, *What a liar!* She
laughs out loud and says, "I don't care what you say, I don't like
these spots. And I *didn't* have them before. Age spots . . .
Here," she says and gives me a hug. "I give them to you."

Sometimes, the oldest people are the youngest at heart—
age spots or no age spots.

EMPATHY

The fragrance always remains in the hand that gives the rose.

HEDA BEJAR

When we become set in our ways, we can become inflexible without even knowing it. Over a lifetime, we grow into habits and ways of thinking as surely as the gardens we plant sink their roots deep into the ground. We begin to believe our way is the only way. We tend our gardens faithfully and pride ourselves on protecting our hearts' careful blossoming from the uprooting power of new ideas or complicated feelings. We'll make a stretch for sympathy, but empathy—empathy is dangerous because it challenges our boundaries, our sense of ourselves.

Empathy requires believing that other people see the world differently than we do. Where sympathy asks the question "How can I help you?" empathy also asks "How can I know you?" Instead of taking someone else's problem and making it our own, we need to go beyond ourselves to see the other person's perspective, to work on a solution that acknowledges *their* identity, not just ours. We may find our gardens forcing strange and wonderful new varieties, amaranthine creations of our hearts. We may learn to understand and accept the people we love in ways impossible to have conceived before.

Empathy is a blossoming evolution of our hearts and minds.

LAST WISH

As to diseases make a habit of two things—
to help, or at least, to do no harm.

HIPPOCRATES

Seventy-five percent of Americans, according to a Gallup survey, believe physicians should have the legal right to "end a patient's life by painless means." In a poll of physicians conducted by the American Society of Internal Medicine, forty percent of doctors interviewed admitted yielding to their patients' pleas to die. As medical technology makes it possible to prolong the process of dying, patients, families, and physicians are confronting issues about death and dying never before faced by the human race.

How and when should we give up the fight for life? What quality of life is worth preserving? And who makes the decision? Should physicians—health care professionals trained throughout history to *do no harm*—help patients to die? Under certain circumstances, is assisting in death inconsistent with doing no harm?

Midway through my father's struggle with colon cancer, he fell into a deep coma caused when the cancer blocked his ureter and toxins from his kidneys backed up in his body. The doctors took our family aside and told us we could let him go, that the coma would give Dad a peaceful death. We refused— as we knew Dad would have himself—even though we knew the tumor was inoperable; a catheter was inserted directly into Dad's kidney. He received radiation treatments and made a miraculous comeback for a period of months, going back to work and on a vacation to London with Mom, before the cancer came back in full force.

But in the last year of his life, Dad was in excruciating pain up to the end. Was that brief interlude worth what followed it? I still look for the answer to that question. I don't know. But it was my family's *choice*.

Choice in dying is a personal right of integrity,
mental and physical.

PUZZLE PIECES

*Nothing puzzles me more than time and space; and yet nothing
troubles me less, as I never think about them.*

CHARLES LAMB, IN A LETTER TO THOMAS MANNING, FEBRUARY 15, 1802

Four cozy tables are always set up outside the dining hall at the retirement community, each with a different puzzle residents work on collaboratively. Once the puzzle is solved, a new one mysteriously appears. These puzzles are big ones, hundreds of pieces strewn over the tables, and no clue as to what pictures will come out in the end. Residents stop by to chat, fit a piece or two, and move on. Mom and I enjoyed watching the puzzles grow. We wondered how many puzzles the retirement community had and how long it would take for them all to circulate among the many apartment complexes and show up again, a little easier this time for the knowing.

Once Mom entered the nursing home at the community, I noticed the puzzles in each floor's activity room. I always took Mom to sit with me while I worked on the puzzles. I'd encourage her to help me: shifting through the pieces was good for her manual dexterity and her mental dexterity, too. For me, the puzzles were a way to fit this difficult time to the high hopes we'd had when Mom bravely moved to the retirement community to start a new chapter in her life. One winter night working on puzzles, Mom sang an entire hymn to me word for word. It was the first time she had strung more than three lucid sentences together, much less an entire verse of a song, in a very long time.

Puzzles often reveal unexpected, beautiful pictures.

MUSICAL CHAIRS

*Family life! The United Nations is child's play compared to the tugs
and splits and need to understand and forgive in any family.*

MAY SARTON

Who takes Mom or Dad?" is a loaded question for their children, full of logistics, medical necessity, finances, and family dynamics—a threshold crossed when a parent's autonomous life in his or her own home can no longer be propped up. Even if there is money to give a parent care in an assisted living community or nursing home, many children believe the cost is just too high—financially and emotionally. They feel the need to give care themselves. Indeed, that's our society's myth of what it means to be a "good child."

I remember Mom telling me about her conversation with Uncle Donald about how they would handle care for their mother after Sylvia had surgery for colon cancer. Sylvia, Mom, and Uncle Donald sat in Mom's kitchen. According to Mom, Sylvia never said a word; she sat and listened to her children talk about her in the third person. *Where is* she *going to stay?* Sylvia stayed with Mom, and Uncle Donald agreed to take care of Sylvia's house and personal business and to provide support for Mom when things got tough. Some siblings will alternate care of a parent until the demands of the care go beyond what can be done at home and require skilled nursing attention. Solutions are as personal as each situation. The fact is, Sylvia didn't want to live with anyone. She had no choices, and she didn't like it any better than her children did. Who would?

We all cling to our need for a sense of place.

HOME CARE

Many hands make light work.

PROVERB

Providing care for an aging, infirm parent in your own home is a full-time job. And it is different from caring for a child. Children are constantly growing, discovering, and incorporating new skills and knowledge. Our parents, however, are becoming more dependent; losing skills and abilities, they must be supported in decline. As this happens, caregiving is ever more demanding and exhausting, both physically and mentally.

If you are providing in-home care for your parent, you need to take full advantage of the resources available to make your life—and your parent's—as easy and comfortable as possible. Find out about adult day-care services in your community. Consider hiring a home health aide to help you with any tasks of daily living that are now difficult for you to manage alone, such as bathing or dressing your parent. Get someone to do housekeeping chores or to cook for you periodically.

As much as you may want to try, you are going to find it next to impossible to care for your parent and your family nonstop, day in, day out. Give yourself some breathing room by arranging for as much supplemental care as you can. Make sure to schedule time in each day—even if it is only fifteen minutes—to do something enjoyable that is just for you, from a ritual cup of tea to watching a favorite program on TV or performing yoga sun salutations on the back porch. It's not selfish to take good care of yourself as well as the ones you love.

When we nurture ourselves, we restore the energy we need to nurture others.

CIRCUMSTANCES

Circumstances! I make circumstances!

NAPOLEON BONAPARTE

We all possess more power than we know to shape each moment of our lives, right now, today. This is the day we can shape and influence. Today is our hope and our promise. Every new hour is an hour of opportunity for change and growth, for problem-solving, and for reaching out.

Whenever you feel powerless in the face of circumstances that seem larger than you are, look for the courage to focus on the individual challenges at hand. Learn to let others help you find effective solutions. Draw on the resources of family, friends, neighbors and community, health care providers, counselors and social workers, legal advisors, financial planners, or others who have experience with the problems you are working on and who can assist you in some way—one challenge at a time.

Together, we can master circumstances!

Marshal your resources. Build a strong network to help support you and your loved ones through life's changing circumstances.

TRANSFERS

True strength is delicate.

Louise Nevelson

If your aging parent or grandparent is using a wheelchair, learn the proper body mechanics for safely performing wheelchair transfers, that is, for helping your loved one to move safely into or out of the wheelchair. The degree to which assistance is required will depend on an elder's own strength, flexibility, and balance. Determination or force of will is not a factor. It is important—for both the elder and the caregiver—to assess physical capabilities realistically and accurately and to work within those limits to avoid falls and injuries (to either of you!) during transfers.

Some important rules for the caregiver: Make sure the wheelchair brakes are locked. To prevent back injury, position yourself close to your loved one during a transfer and plant both feet hip-distance apart to create a balanced center of gravity. If possible, you should both be wearing rubber-soled or flat shoes (heels are not transfer-friendly attire). Move obstacles out of the way and position the elder so that the transfer takes place on the elder's strongest side. Bending from the hips and knees, place your hands on the elder's waist—lifting from the arms or armpits could cause injury to your loved one. Ask the elder to place his or her hands on the armrest of the wheelchair; arms placed around your neck during a transfer could drag you off balance. Together, push up to a standing position. Still holding on with a firm grip, pivot the elder safely and lower into a seated position on a chair, sofa, or bed. Take your time. Give the elder (and yourself!) a chance to rest after the transfer is completed.

The same basic procedures apply for helping someone into or out of a car. I always have to look around for my grandmother, Jessie, after helping her out of a car seat. Before I can close the car door and gather up any packages we've accumulated, she's already on the move. Watch for an elder's strength, balance, color, and breathing if he or she decides to walk for any distance—even a short one. If your loved one seems unsteady or looks ill, slow down and find the first available seat. Go back and sit in the car again if you have to. Better safe than sorry.

Loving, steady movements take us where we need to go.

A LITTLE HELP

Intimate relationships cannot substitute for a life plan. But to have any meaning or viability at all, a life plan must include intimate relationships.

HARRIET LERNER

Jessie, at eighty-eight, is the perfect candidate for an assisted living community. Every time I talk to Gram's geriatrician about her health, he hammers home the fact that Jessie needs social contact—that it is as important as any drug he might prescribe or any health problem we might solve. "I like my own home," Jessie asserts, "I've been here thirty-five years, almost as long as you've been alive; I don't pay any rent and I don't answer to anybody." All good points. Yet she craves *people*; she is desperate for connection with the world outside her windows. She's so stubborn, though. She'll talk about it—mainly in the context of *I don't want to be a burden to my family no one is going to take care of me when the time comes I'm ready* kind of thing. Gram confuses assisted living facilities with nursing homes.

Assisted living is a relatively new alternative that provides support for older people who are still active but who may find the responsibilities of maintaining a home overwhelming and for whom the activities of daily living are growing to be more of a challenge. Like a college dormitory, residents have their own rooms, furnished with their own belongings. Meals are served in a community dining room. Housekeeping services are provided. Health aides administer medication to residents who need help in taking their medicines promptly and correctly, and a physician is on call should a medical emergency arise. Rooms, hallways, and common areas are designed to be elder-friendly—with grab bars in the bathrooms and sometimes seats built into the showers, emergency pull cords, wall guard rails, carpeted floors, and sturdy chairs to help prevent falls. There are no steps to climb up or down and no long distances to walk. Your parent is in a safe, supported environment where life can be enjoyed and hassles and responsibilities are taken care of by staff.

Most important, assisted living arrangements provide social contact and stimulation without the effort and concerns of traveling out of the house or the stress and loneliness of waiting for visitors who will stay only a short time. Your parent or grandparent will be surrounded with people every day, making new friends and participating in an active community. Sure, it may be hard for them to give up the familiarity and autonomy of their own homes. Some people believe it is dangerous to move loved ones so late in life, to change everything. On the other hand, the precious gift of human contact and friendship is vital to sustaining our health, hearts, and souls. What good is a house if you are isolated?

A home is a place that meets our needs, growing and changing with us.

ALBUM

You as a child; how pretty. How people change; still,
I would know you anywhere.

ROSE MACAULAY

In Mom's room at the nursing home, I've surrounded her with pictures of her favorite times—my brother and me as kids at Christmas, huge grins in a room filled with gifts, grandparents, and an enormous tree; antics with Mom and Dad and Mike, Uncle Sam and Aunt Marie on the beach in Ocean City; our graduations from college, the first in the family; Mom and Dad on a white sand beach in Hawaii; Mom and Dad dressed as Wilma Flintstone and Betty Rubble for a Halloween party. While Mom could still tell me, I'd ask her to relate the stories of these pictures to me, as well as other good times remembered. Later, as the symptoms of dementia began to overtake her mind, I would tell the stories of the pictures to Mom, heartened when she contributed a detail or laughed with recognition.

There is one picture, taken last year, of my brother and me at his home in California. "Isn't that good," Mom said when I brought it to her. Taking the frame in her arms, she holds the picture close to her heart.

Our pictures honor our lives: a trail of memory fixed in time.

SELF-IMAGE

Biographies are but the clothes and buttons of the man. . . .

MARK TWAIN

Choosing appropriate clothing becomes harder for an aging person who may have trouble reaching for a back zipper, pulling on hose or trousers, doing buttons, or tying shoes. For a person experiencing mental confusion, even remembering how to dress may be challenging. The frustration of not looking and feeling the way they want, with the ease they are used to, can be devastating to elders' self-images.

We can help by gently suggesting subtle adjustments: Velcro fasteners, sweaters with one or two large buttons in the front, slip-on rubber-soled shoes, elasticized pants or skirts that simply pull up. But we can also help by assisting an older person in looking and feeling the way they remember themselves through subtle but important touches such as make-up, a manicure, a good haircut, or the scent of a favorite after-shave or perfume. For a person in a nursing home, a purse or a wallet filled with gum or candy, loose change, family photos, and some tissues can hold great value. It is important to be sensitive to the small details of grooming and dress that make elders feel good about themselves.

Respect the dignity of an elder's self-image.

MISS JEAN AND MOM

Friendship is a sheltering tree.

Samuel Taylor Coleridge, "Youth and Age"

Miss Jean and Mom met on their first jobs after high school at a Baltimore furniture showroom. By coincidence years later, they met in the supermarket and discovered that they'd bought houses on the same street. The two have been fast friends ever since. My brother, Mike, and I grew up with Miss Jean as a kind of second mother. I particularly remember being dragged as a child on shopping trips with Miss Jean and Mom—endless excursions from the dressing rooms to the sales floor: "I need this skirt in a ten in navy." "Hon, bring me those slacks in a twelve in khaki." One time, Miss Jean and Mom, heading back to the parking lot after a shopping trip, found an elephant tethered next to Mom's car; apparently, the circus was in town. "Your mother wouldn't go anywhere near that car. She just stood on the curb and handed me the keys!" Miss Jean tells me, laughing.

I ask Miss Jean how she feels to see her best friend in a nursing home. "Sad," she says, "and angry. Your mother wouldn't talk about things. I told your mother everything, but she kept too much bottled up inside. She wouldn't talk about your brother being gay. She wouldn't talk about being sick. And you know, your mother and I were together when she first discovered something might be wrong, but we didn't know it was Parkinson's. We were eating lunch and your mother's little finger on her right hand was bending back funny and we couldn't figure out why. . . . That was in 1975. Maybe if Gloria had been more open, she could have helped herself more.

She didn't try hard enough; she just let things go." Amen, Miss Jean. "The last time I went up to the nursing home, I fed your mother lunch, and you know what she said to me? She said, 'I've been waiting for someone to feed me all my life.' Can you believe it?" Yes, Miss Jean, I can believe it. Mom always wanted someone else to make everything all right.

About five years ago or so, I convinced Mom to check into Hopkins for a week to reevaluate her Parkinson's. The symptoms were showing despite Mom's insistence on denying or ignoring her balance problems and growing mental confusion. Mom fought me every step of the way and only grudgingly agreed to go through with it. Mom and Miss Jean both still lived in their houses on Kirkwood Road back then. Miss Jean went with us for the hospital admission and stayed with us the whole day. In the parking lot, ready to go home, Miss Jean slipped her arm around me and we stood, fighting back tears.

Our friends for life know us so well, better than we know ourselves.

LET IT RAIN

Let it rain down love. . . . Love, love, love, and sunshowers.

James Taylor, "Shower the People"

My grandmother, Jessie, always says, "Live according to the weather. When it starts to rain, put up an umbrella." Sometimes life seems overwhelming. So many things to do, obligations to meet, responsibilities to honor. When we are working, maintaining a home, caring for our children *and* for our parents or grandparents, there often seems to be no end in sight and no time for ourselves. We wonder when the storm will ever end and we long for the warm sun of a lazy day. How can we stop the rain?

When it starts to rain, put up an umbrella. A simple, logical thing to do. We may not be able to stop the rain—let it come. But we *can* seek protection in the loving embrace of our families, the memory of good times we've had and, with a collective strength, move forward *together* toward clearer skies.

Love provides a powerful shelter under threatening skies.

SPEND DOWN

Abstractions hardened into the concrete: even death is a purchase.

Nadine Gordimer

Mom never thought her Parkinson's would catch up with her. She expected to live the rest of her life in her one-bedroom, independent living apartment at the retirement community, never needing nursing home care—at least, maybe, not until the very end. I knew the truth would probably be something very different: Early on, I considered the likely prospect that Mom would need care in the community's assisted living and/or nursing home facilities and that her savings would be used up to pay for her long-term health care.

I toured the community's assisted living and nursing home facilities (without Mom, who refused to look at them) and I hired a lawyer to read the community's entrance contract to make sure we understood what we agreed to, legally and financially. At the retirement community, Mom's autonomous life could continue, her health supported and her care in a quality nursing home assured even when the money was gone and Medicaid kicked in.

Remember, Medicare and Medicaid are not the same. Medicare pays only toward doctor and hospital expenses for over sixty-fivers. Medicaid is health assistance for the poor; you must apply for it and meet the government's strict eligibility requirements to receive benefits toward nursing home care. The only instance in which Medicare will pay on a limited basis for nursing home care is one that qualifies as "restorative" therapy, and usually applies to a temporary condition. Unfortunately, I was right about Mom's situation; she is spending down her personal assets to qualify for Medicaid. While it seems like such a waste, I know Mom is lucky. My father's lifework has purchased quality end-of-life care for Mom. And for that, our whole family is grateful.

Foresight is the master builder:
The blueprints we design in the present give
us the plans of choice for the future.

THE GOOD CHILD

I wonder if we could contrive . . . some magnificent myth that
would in itself carry conviction to our whole community.

PLATO

*H*ow can good children "put" their parents in nursing homes? Our
society holds that good children should provide their
parents' care—the same way the two-parent nuclear family is
offered as a panacea, a cure for all ills and a solution for all
difficulties. The fact is this: In the trenches of everyday life,
we grapple hand-to-hand with the profound moral, bioethical,
and practical issues of taking care of our parents and our families. The dilemma of providing responsible care is one un-
solvable by love or blood alone.

Our collective guilt, our cultural myth of discarded age,
usually portrays nursing homes as places of neglect where
children abandon their parents. But if a parent requires round-
the-clock skilled nursing care, choosing a good licensed nursing home can be the compassionate act of a loving child.
Would I rather my mother were not in a nursing home? Of
course. Do I like our situation? No.

If your parent needs care beyond what can be provided at
home with the help of adult day care or home health aides,
nursing homes are a viable alternative. So you don't have to keep
trying to be your parent's nurse as well as your parent's child.

We are all good children, making tough choices every day
to get the best, appropriate care for our parents.

FOOD FOR THOUGHT

Eating is touch carried to the bitter end.

Samuel Butler

I am sitting in the nursing home cafeteria, feeding dinner—turkey and vegetables—to my mother. Mom seems to forget she is eating, holding food in her mouth or not sucking up on a straw to take fluids. When I call her name, it takes a lot longer than usual to bring her back to animation and focus her attention on eating, sometimes a whole minute or more. I used to compare this to feeding a child, but it's completely different. While a child's brain is proliferating synaptic connections, an exploration that sculpts the growing mind, my mother is the victim of "faulty wiring," her nervous system a damaged phone cord that interrupts interrupts reconnects interrupts, connecting and disconnecting unpredictably.

Panicky, I try to get Mom to tell me if she likes the food. Maybe, I think, the neural connection is doomed because the taste is unpleasant. "Do you want ice cream instead?" I ask her. Mom's brows knit together. She turns to me in utter bewilderment and confusion. I say it several times gently: *Ice cream, ice cream, ice cream, do you want ice cream . . .*

Mom answers me, "I can't get it out." To hear and not be able to respond; to desire to move yet remain fixed.

The person you love is there still,
somewhere deep within a failing mind and body.

EMERGENCY

She had the loaded handbag of someone who camps out and seldom goes home, or who imagines life must be full of emergencies.

MAVIS GALLANT

"Your grandmother wants you to take her to the emergency room," my friend Diane tells me. It is New Year's Eve. I have just arrived in Baltimore from New York to spend the holiday, and I'm staying at Diane's apartment. I ask Diane if she is kidding. Apparently not. Gram started calling Diane about the time she knew I'd be hitting the New Jersey Turnpike. "Tell my granddaughter I'm sick and I need to go to the hospital. No, I don't want you to take me. No, I don't want an ambulance. My granddaughter can take me when she gets here. I want to wait until she gets here. It's only another hour or so."

I get to Gram's house and she is dressed and ready to go. She seems fine. "Why do you need to go to the hospital?" I ask her. "Did you call your doctor?"

"I called him and he said I should make an appointment for right after the holiday. But I'm not going to do that. I've got to find out what's wrong with me. I need to go to the hospital to get checked out." And so my aunt Mary and I take Jessie to the emergency room at Johns Hopkins. *She's over eighty*, I say to myself. *I have to take this seriously no matter what.* I call my brother, Mike, in California and he agrees.

It turns out, after many hours, an ECG, and several X rays, that all Jessie needed was an acid blocker for indigestion. What really happened here? Mike and I believe that Jessie was lonely because I had spent my first Christmas away from Baltimore with Mike in Los Angeles; Gram wanted to let us know we had to be ready for anything. Jessie, however, believes my Christmas with Mike in California had nothing to do with anything. "I felt sick and my own grandchildren gave me a hard time about taking me to the emergency room," she says.

There are many different kinds of emergencies. We need to pay attention to them all.

The aching heart has its own urgency.

PRAYER

Prayer does not use up artificial energy,
doesn't burn up any fossil fuel, doesn't pollute.

Margaret Mead

Prayer can be the most powerful force on earth. Harnessing the power of prayer means creating a laser beam of positive energy that educates and transforms us at the same time it benefits the objects of our prayers. In a study of 393 heart patients at San Francisco General Hospital, half the patients were prayed for and half were not. No one—patients, families, or health care professionals—knew which patients received the prayers. At the end of the study, patients with prayer power had fewer complications and needed less antibiotics. Other research studies are revealing the same results.

Many of us are out of practice or have difficulty praying. Prayer could be just a faded childhood memory of a mealtime grace and bedtime verse. Or perhaps you have trouble with the idea of a Supreme Being. Or maybe you see prayer as a selfish and desperate act people resort to when they need a favor. Think about prayer in a different way. Pray for the health and joy of your loved ones, of the people you pass on the street, of humanity. On waking, give a prayer of thanks for the priceless opportunity to participate in the amazing gift of life. Offer one positive thought each day as an affirmation of the energy, resilience, and joy of the human spirit. Share your prayers with your parents or grandparents.

Open our hearts and our hands to healing and joy for ourselves and
for every living being. May our every breath say "Yes" to life.

FUNERAL TRUST

Do you realize the planning that goes into a death? Probably even more than goes into a marriage. This, after all, really is for eternity.

GAIL PARENT

Setting up a funeral trust for Mom was one of the hardest tasks I've had to perform to ensure her best interests. The law makes it possible for individuals to create irrevocable pre-need funeral service trusts. You pay an amount to the funeral home in advance to cover the cost of the funeral and burial and the funeral home puts this money into a trust, which accrues interest. The trust cannot be touched until the death of the person named as its grantor. If and when your loved one applies for Medicaid, the funeral trust is exempt from consideration as an asset.

Mom's finances reached the crisis point where I had to invoke the financial power of attorney to set up such a trust or lose the money for Mom's funeral to the Medicaid spend-down process. The whole thing felt cruel, as if the system asked me to bury Mom alive. And I was angry at Mom for not having the courage and foresight to have made these arrangements years ago herself when she was healthy enough to do it.

As the funeral director read off the standard costs of burial, I thought hard to remember whether Mom loved orchids or hated them. I stood in the casket room to pick out a coffin and my brain shut down. Only an hour ago, I'd sat with Mom in the nursing home's dining room feeding her lunch. *This can't be happening,* I told myself. *I don't want to do this.* But I did do it—I picked out a coffin just as I had ten years ago for my father when Mom was too befuddled to make the decision. All at once, everything seemed so clear—Mom left the tough choices to me, and from her weakness I inherited a strength. What seemed a betrayal I suddenly knew as an act of compassion and care.

Our choices make us human.

READING

*I think I was born with the impression that what happened
in books was much more reasonable, and interesting, and real,
in some ways, than what happened in life.*

ANNE TYLER

Next to shopping, reading is my mother's passion. She gets it from her mother. When Sylvia died, my uncle cleaned out a cache of books in a back storeroom in her house, hundreds of paperback romances and celebrity biographies stacked against a wall, meticulously arranged according to size and subject. That was Sylvia.

Early on, Mom instilled in me a great curiosity for stories. Books marveled us. By the time I was in junior high school, Mom and I brought home a shopping bag of books a week from the library and traded them: Herman Wouk, F. Scott Fitzgerald, the Brontë sisters, James Michener. When I went to college, I brought home Eudora Welty, J. D. Salinger, William Faulkner, Virginia Woolf, Vladimir Nabokov. Somehow, though, I think Mom still preferred an evening with the latest James Clavell, but she humored me.

Mom found it harder and harder to read as her illness progressed. First, we tried large-print books—you can get almost anything in large print these days—but her eye muscles were affected by the Parkinson's, and she couldn't concentrate on the page. We tried books on tape, using a Fisher-Price tape player designed for toddlers, but Mom's growing confusion made this hard as well. She'd lose her place, jam the tapes, or just forget and wander off. In the nursing home, the charge nurse told me, "She'll be talking, and for a long time we

140

couldn't figure out what she was talking *about*—and then one day we realized she was trying to read anything she saw that had writing on it." This is Mom.

Now, in the end stages of Parkinson's, Mom's ability to converse and communicate is slipping away. Not knowing what else to do, I read to her. The sound of my voice reading the words soothes us both. Once again, we conspire to enter the world of a book together. "Okay, Mom, *The Bridges of Madison County*. They made this one into a movie with Clint Eastwood and Meryl Streep. I hear it's a good story. . . ."

I read: *There are songs that come free from the blue-eyed grass, from the dust of a thousand country roads. This is one of them.*

Words help us to feel with our minds,
to make sense of our world with a story shared.

QUALITY OF LIFE

To cure sometimes, to relieve often, to comfort always.

FIFTEENTH-CENTURY FRENCH FOLK SAYING

My mother, in the end stages of Parkinson's, is bedridden. Her body is stiff and unyielding. She is incontinent of urine and bowel. She has difficulty eating and swallowing. Her mind is incapable of holding sustained intelligent discourse, though she knows the people around her and still comments on her surroundings. "I want to go out," Mom said one evening when the nursing home staff suggested bringing Mom dinner in her room. We went through the laborious process of getting Mom into the dining room, feeding her, and putting her back to bed after which Mom sank into a deep, exhausted sleep.

My mom was diagnosed with Parkinson's more than twenty years ago when I was in high school. Sinemet was a new drug then, a miracle drug in the eyes of Parkinson's patients, and my mom is one of the first to use this drug therapy effectively over so long a period of time. Because of Sinemet (Carbidopa/Levodopa), Mom functioned for fifteen years with little interference from the Parkinson's. "No one would ever know that anything is wrong," she'd say proudly. But now the drug that saved her life is helping to prolong her dying with a quality of life that, to my mind, is horrible to contemplate and harder still to endure. Yet my mother clings to her life, tenacious in illness. I sit with her, hold her hand, and wait. The medical assistant arrives with the next dose of Sinemet. What do we do when miracles turn into nightmares?

Our hearts are left to bear what the body cannot.

ONE DAY AT A TIME

I cannot forget my mother. Though not as sturdy as others,
she is my bridge. When I needed to get across,
she steadied herself long enough for me to run across safely.

RENITA WEEMS

I can't confide in Mom; I can't worry her with what's happening in my life. Because Mom can't understand me anymore. I miss her. She still knows me. She's still able to speak a sentence and focus on a simple idea. But there are no more heart-to-heart talks—only *I love you* or *You need a new pair of shoes* or *You look tired* or *You look beautiful.*

I tuck the coverlet knitted by the retirement community's sewing circle snugly around Mom's shoulders and chatter on about this and that, nothing important. My touchstone is silent, her expression unresponsive, staring. But my love reaches down to find Mom in the heartbeat where she lives, still, and I know she is cheering me on, lifting me up. Helping me face life's problems, every day, one day at a time.

A heartbeat does more than measure life—
its rhythm holds the voice of love.

MAY 1981

*Some memories are realities, and are better
than anything that can ever happen to one again.*

WILLA CATHER

May 1981: Mom's perfect time. My brother, Mike, lived in New York, enjoying a successful career in advertising. I graduated from college that month. Both hitting fifty, with their children educated, our parents looked forward to traveling and to having a good time. Dad started talking about taking early retirement at fifty-five. The view from the catbird seat looked fine. But in October that year, Dad was diagnosed with cancer; he died at fifty-four.

Paging through Mom's medical records at the nursing home on my most recent visit, I came across a cognitive evaluation for the Parkinson's done about a year or so ago, when Mom could still write. She struggled determinedly through the questions to the last one, which asked her to write a sentence. Mom wrote: *I want to go home.* Knowing Mom, I understood what she meant: Let this all be a dream. Heal me by sending me back to Kirkwood Road. Let me stay safe, right there in a perpetual May 1981.

*Time collapses upon our minds with the force
—and elusiveness—
of waves crashing to the shore.*

IN MEMORY

What interests me most is neither still life nor landscape,
but the human figure. It is through it that I best succeed in expressing
the almost religious feeling I have towards life.

HENRI MATISSE

My brother, Mike, and I talk about what we'll do when Mom dies. It is new ground for us both. Ten years ago, we came to Dad's funeral from vastly different perspectives. Mike hadn't agreed with Mom's decision to honor Dad's wish to die at home; Mike thought a hospital was the appropriate place with the best resources for care. He didn't think that Mom, Gram, and I should take on the task of caring for Dad in the last weeks, even with the help of a hospice nurse.

To me at the time, it didn't make any difference where Dad was, as long as I could be with him. Unlike Mom's situation in the nursing home now, where she needs skilled nursing care around the clock but is not in imminent danger of death, we all knew then that Dad could not be sustained, that caring for him was not really an act of maintenance but a last act of love.

Mike came down to see Dad, to say good-bye. Only now do I realize how hard it must have been for them: Dad and Mike had a difficult relationship; they didn't agree on anything, including this death. And Mike wouldn't give in about it like I did. At the funeral, Mike and I couldn't help each other; we were like people standing on different sides of a fence. It stayed that way for a long time.

When Mom dies, after a Catholic funeral in accordance with her faith, Mike and I plan to go to the Baltimore Museum of Art, just us two, to honor our mother by walking through the famous Cone collection of Matisse. Mom loved Matisse, whose art was joy, who saw each of his pictures as a birth bringing forth, in his own words, "a new face into the representation of the world through the human spirit." Mike and I will transform our grief, together this time, in a rebirth of joy and wonder. We know it's the right thing to do.

There are always flowers for those who want to see them.

SOMETHING BORROWED

True love is like ghosts, which everybody talks about and few have seen.

FRANÇOIS DE LA ROCHEFOUCAULD

As anyone who has ever sold a house will agree, one of the hardest parts is going through the attic. A few years ago, when I helped Mom sell the house on Kirkwood Road—the house she raised her family in—I found anything and everything: old newspapers, lawn furniture, my recital outfits from ballet class, my brother's college papers. I found pictures of old times, of relatives I have never met and will never know. And the love letters my father wrote to my mother from Korea as a Marine during the war. Mom cried when I offered them to her. "You keep them," she said. Scores of letters in crumbling envelopes bearing the handwriting I knew so well. Mom left me with the letters still in my outstretched hands. *What do I do with these?* I sat in the attic reading about Dad's hopes and dreams for his future with Mom and then sealed them in a new box, which lived at the back of Mom's bedroom closet at the retirement community.

When Mom moved from her independent living apartment to the community's nursing home facility, the box surfaced again. Now that box of love letters lives in the back of my closet at the bottom of a garment bag that also holds Mom's wedding dress. I will not break the seal—that is for the next generation.

Some things we save because they do not belong to us,
but pass from our parents to our children.

TOWARD ADVENTURE

I am walking in Chinatown in New York City with my good friend Laura and her parents. Canal Street is packed with every sort of person. Savvy New Yorkers that we are, Laura and I weave through the crowd, looking back over our shoulders to see if her parents are keeping up all right. Has the city overtaken them? Laura's parents are only a few steps behind us, and her mom's eyes are filled with amusement. "Don't worry about *us*," she says, "We've got our eyes on *you*." Laura and I laugh, surprised.

Even as our parents age, they are still looking out for us. Whether they age with robust vitality or whether they succumb to illness or infirmity, their parenting impulses don't go away. We can look forward to life's adventures knowing that the support and encouragement of our parents will always accompany us, if only in spirit or memory.

Laura and I turn to look forward, where anything can happen.

We carry our parents' love forward to new adventures.

Appendix 1: Important Papers

*The historian, essentially, wants more documents than he can really use;
the dramatist only wants more liberties than he can really take.*

Henry James

It is a good idea for your parent or grandparent to locate important papers and place them in a locked box in a safe place in the house. For insurance cards or identification that your loved one uses regularly, place photocopies in the box. You might also want to hold onto a complete set of photocopied documents, especially if you live in a different town or state from your parent.

Here's a list of the kind of papers you'll want to keep track of:

* Social Security card

* Health insurance policy and card,
   disability insurance policy

* Medicare and/or Medicaid cards

* Bank account numbers

* Investment accounts or stocks held

* Pension fund information and group number

* Life insurance policies

* Tax returns

* Birth certificates for both parents,
   citizenship papers

* Marriage license

* Divorce papers

* Military service records, including discharge papers

* Death certificate (if spouse is deceased)

* House deed and title, mortgage papers, leases, homeowner's or rental insurance policies

* Auto title, registration, and insurance policy

* Driver's license or DMV photo ID card

* Durable power of attorney for legal and financial matters

* Living will/Durable power of attorney for health care

* Pre-need funeral trust document or funeral insurance policy, cemetery plot deed

* Last will and testament

* If in a retirement community, assisted living facility, or nursing home, the original resident and care contract

Appendix 2: Nursing Home Checklist

Make no judgments where you have no compassion.

Anne McCaffrey

Choosing the right nursing home requires patience, commitment, and doing a lot of homework. As government supervision increases, nursing home care is improving. Don't assume that all nursing homes are alike, or that they are staffed and equipped to provide the best care for your parent's individual needs. This is by no means meant to be an all-inclusive checklist, but simply a place to begin. Create a research notebook, adding your questions and recording your findings as you visit facilities to choose the right one for your parent's care.

✲ Contact the ombudsman at your state's agency on aging to find out what appropriate facilities are located in your area. Make sure the facilities you consider all have active, valid licenses to operate. Obtain copies of the government inspection reports of facilities—available either directly from the facility or from your state's department of human services or appropriate state agency. You can also check on homes with the office of consumer affairs and your local Better Business Bureau. Are the facilities JCAHO certified?

✲ Arrange for a tour of each nursing home, then visit them yourself unannounced at different times of the day—that way you'll see how care is provided during meals, in the afternoon, on weekends, or after residents' bedtimes. Talk to residents and their family members about the quality of care provided. Eat the food typically served to residents. A low occupancy rate, under ninety percent, could signal problems.

✳ Are rooms, hallways, and common areas comfortably clean and orderly? Are residents encouraged to have their own possessions in their rooms? How are residents dressed? Notice what staff members are doing: Are they interacting with residents? With each other? Are they performing a task or just standing around? Do staff make you feel welcome, readily providing information and addressing your questions and concerns? Do staff encourage residents to make independent decisions?

✳ Ask about the training, certification, and licensure of staff who will provide care to your parent. Does the nursing home qualify for Medicare and Medicaid as a "skilled nursing facility"? (Some facilities choose not to accept such compensation for monetary reasons.) How many residents live at the home? How many Medicaid beds does the facility provide? Find out the ratio of patients to health care providers on both day and evening shifts. Ask about the rate of staff turnover broken down by job description.

✳ Is the nursing home affiliated with a hospital or physician network? What kind of physician or specialist care (dentists, ophthalmologists, podiatrists, etc.) is available to your parent through the nursing home? How often do doctors make rounds to visit residents? Is the physician's care plan shared with residents and their families?

✳ Do allied health professionals provide care at the nursing home? Allied health staff provide supplemental care and include occupational and physical therapists, speech pathologists, nutritionists, social workers, and recreational therapists.

✲ Are ambulating residents offered activities off-site? Ask for a calendar listing events and activities regularly planned for residents. Examine the outdoor space available to residents. It should be easily accessible and, if the weather is nice, occupied.

✲ Are there volunteer programs and does the home have good relationships with community organizations, especially schools and local businesses?

✲ Does the facility devote space to residents who are experiencing dementia or who require some kind of special assistance?

✲ Are there hidden costs of care, such as laundry, prescription drugs, or transportation to off-site doctor's visits? Are up-front fees required to enter the nursing home? To what extent can your parent control his or her own financial affairs? You can't ask enough questions about money and finances.

✲ You'll want to know the nursing home's philosophy on the use of restraints for patients who may fall or otherwise injure themselves if able to move about unsupervised.

✲ Find out the nursing home's philosophy on end-of-life care—you want to choose a facility where you feel assured that your parent's treatment decisions at end-of-life will be clearly honored and followed.

Resources

ABLEDATA
8455 Colesville Road, Suite 935
Silver Spring, Maryland 20910
(800) 227-0216
Web site: http://www.abledata.com
Database of manufacturers of assistive devices and
rehabilitation equipment—from reachers to wheelchairs
to voice-activated computer systems

American Association of Retired Persons
601 E Street, NW
Washington, DC 20049
(202) 434-2277 * (800) 424-3410
All-purpose information on elder care topics

American Bar Association
Commission on Legal Problems of the Elderly
740 15th Street
Washington, DC 20005
(202) 662-1000
Information on legal issues specific to elders

Center for Medical Consumers
237 Thompson Street
New York, New York
(212) 674-7105
Research and consumer advocacy organization with
medical library; publishes newsletter *HealthFacts*

CHILDREN OF AGING PARENTS
1609 Woodborne Road
Woodborne Office Campus, Suite 302-A
Levittown, Pennsylvania 19057
(215) 345-5104 * (800) 227-7297
Information on elder care topics, referrals for geriatric
care managers, housing options, and legal issues

CHOICE IN DYING
200 Varick Street, 10th Floor
New York, New York 10014
(212) 366-5540 * (800) 989-9455
Information on living wills and durable
powers of attorney for health care

ELDERHOSTEL
75 Federal Street
Boston, Massachusetts 02110
(617) 426-7788
Publishes catalogs of travel and educational opportunities
for seniors—United States, Canada,
International, and Service/Humanities editions

HEALTHFINDER
U.S. Department of Health and Human Services
Web site: http://www.healthfinder.gov
Links to over 500 health information Web sites,
databases, publications, and on-line bulletin boards

HEALTH INSURANCE ASSOCIATION OF AMERICA
555 13th Street NW, Suite 600 East
Washington, DC 20004
(202) 824-1600
Life, health, auto, and property insurance information

HEARING HELPLINE
Better Hearing Institute
P.O. Box 1840
Washington, DC 20013
(800) 327-9355
Information and referrals to local resources, such as
audiologists and organizations for the hearing impaired

HEAR MORE PRODUCTS
P.O. Box 3413
Farmingdale, New York 11735
(800) 881-4327 V/TTY
Catalog of products for persons with
mild to severe hearing loss

THE LIGHTHOUSE NATIONAL CENTER FOR VISION AND AGING
111 East 59th Street
New York, New York 10022
(800) 334-5497
Information on eye care and vision loss,
referrals to local resources

MEDICARE HOTLINE
HEALTH CARE FINANCING ADMINISTRATION
U.S. Department of Health and Human Services
(800) 638-6833
Information on Medicare coverage of mammograms,
Medigap insurance, HMOs, insurance claims,
insurance fraud, general information, and special benefits

NATIONAL ASSOCIATION OF AREA AGENCIES ON AGING
Eldercare Locator
(800) 677-1116
Referrals and information
for local resources nationwide

NATIONAL ASSOCIATION FOR HOME CARE
228 7th Street SE
Washington, DC 20003
(202) 547-7424
Information on choosing a home care provider

NATIONAL ASSOCIATION FOR PROFESSIONAL
GERIATRIC CARE MANAGERS
1604 N. Country Club Road
Tucson, AZ 85716
(520) 881-8008
Information on choosing
a geriatric care manager

NATIONAL INSTITUTE ON AGING
Information Center
P.O. Box 8057
Gaithersburg, Maryland 20898
(800) 222-2225
National Institutes of Health's clearinghouse
on aging and geriatric health care

NATIONAL INSTITUTES OF HEALTH
(301) 496-4000
Web site: http://www.nih.gov

NATIONAL LIBRARY OF MEDICINE
U.S. Department of Health and Human Services
Building 38A, Room 3N-305
8600 Rockville Pike
Bethesda, Maryland 20894
(301) 496-1131
Publishes free directory of health-related
organizations with 800 numbers nationwide

OMBUDSMEN OFFICES
State Agencies on Aging or Departments of Human Services
Contact your state agency to speak with the
ombudsmen in your local area. General information
on elder services, resources, and facilities

PRINCETON UNIVERSITY ELDERCARE
CONTACT RESOURCE GUIDE
Web site: http://www.princeton.edu/main/elder.html

SELF HELP FOR HARD OF HEARING PEOPLE, INC.
7910 Woodmont Avenue, Suite 1200
Bethesda, Maryland 20814
(301) 657-2248 V * (301) 657-2249 TTY
Information on hearing loss,
referrals to local resources

SOCIAL SECURITY
(800) 772-1213
Web site: http://www.ssa.gov/programs/programs_intro.html
General information, Medicare enrollment,
Medicare replacement cards

UNITED SENIORS HEALTH COOPERATIVE
1331 H Street, NW, #500
Washington, DC 20005-4706
(202) 393-6222
General information,
newsletter, catalog of books
and tapes aimed at
aging consumers

U. S. GOVERNMENT PRINTING OFFICE
Superintendent of Documents
P.O. Box 371954
Pittsburgh, Pennsylvania 15250-7954
(202) 512-1800 Telephone
(202) 512-2250 Fax
Write or fax for free catalog of hundreds
of government publications

VISITING NURSES' ASSOCIATION OF AMERICA
3801 East Florida Avenue, Suite 900
Denver, Colorado 80210
(800) 426-2547
Referrals to local visiting nurse
resources for home care